Holistic Philosophical Studies
Presents

Privatization of Local Government

Part 3 in the Series for the Capitalist Element of the Square

by,

Michael Stansfield

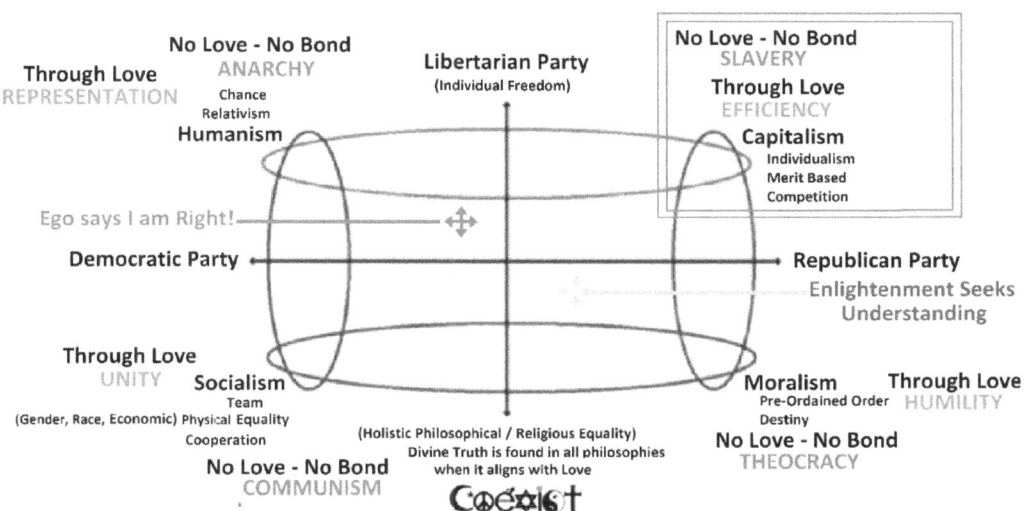

© Holistic Philosophical Studies presents Privatization of Local Government Part 3 in the Series for the Capitalist Element of the Square, October 3, 2024, Michael Stansfield
ISBN: 978-1-300-87773-8

TABLE OF CONTENTS

Laissez-Faire for the Capitalist
Struggles with Capitalism……… 1
Republic to Democracy………… 7
People vs. Ideas………………… 14
Economics of City Gov………… 18
Macroeconomics………………… 21
The Wizard of Oz………………… 25
The City Lord and Budget……. 32
The Underdog…………………… 37
Shire Judges…………………… 41
The Shire Fellowship…………… 45
Spring Cleaning………………… 54
Social Stock Market…………… 56
The Federal Budget…………… 63
National Projects……………… 68
Economization of Socialism….. 73

No customer is worse than no customer.
 -*Joe Albertson*

...for the Capitalist

Laissez-Faire

Privatization of Government

Part III – (Dedicated to the Capitalist Element of the Square)

Why Humanity Struggles with Capitalism

In the first section I stressed the importance of equality among the diversity of political and religious opinions and followed with the previous section through a blueprint for a direct democracy so that a legislature of "We the People" may be conceived through a practical and common-sense foundation. Yet as we look to the private sector, we must acknowledge that capitalism is not democratic. The relationship between employer and employee is not equitable. If the employee is to eat, they must become the slave of an employer, or risk it all to leap the ever-widening gulf from employee to employer. Ninety percent of startups perish in the attempt, yet these entrepreneurs who attempted to break their shackles were also slaves to their dreams, may they rest in peace. If corporations were democratic institutions and the resources equally divided there would be no incentive for anyone to work harder than anyone else and if pay was determined through popular vote as each person believed they deserved which enterprise would last more than a few days before becoming insolvent? It is important to understand the concept of working on another's passion on the psyche of the human spirit. My father once told me the hardest part of each day is just getting out of bed in the morning. In most surveys the person people typically hate the most is there boss because they impede on our liberty as to how we imagine the enterprise should be run and our own impression of how tasks should be performed. And from the perspective of many managers attempting to please everyone is as frustrating as herding cats. Yet while doing the work others deem to be our priority is drudgery, even our own tasks outside of work is a source of dread. That "To do list" of things that never seems to get done, such as, cleaning out the garage, writing that memoir, finishing that project in the backyard. It is human nature to prefer rest over work and all things being equal to have others complete our own tasks. An irony of a body and mind that longs for rest and relaxation in competition with a human spirit that always compels us to desire more. The weakness of the body and mind continually worn down by time, over a human spirit through which time perpetually opens our mind to new horizons.

The conservative rightly points out the need for the dominant position of the employer over the employee because work in part involves compulsion and without compulsion, if all your needs were provided without the necessity to work for it everyone would stay home, toss the alarm clock, and sleep in, and production would fall to that of the neanderthal era. What the conservative fails to understand is that the same laziness among employees that necessitates a form of management over them also impairs that management because management is also impaired by the same vices as all human beings to take advantage of their situation. Even communism had its own form of management, and it didn't take long for everyone to want to be management, and no one wanted to be among the workers. The employee is held in check, some may say even restrained, by the employer, but the employer check on their behavior is held through the Board of Directors. Because the CEO is paid through stock options, if the CEO is successful over the course of several years their stockholdings become large enough that during the vote for the Board of Directors the CEO has a large sway in who is represented on the board. Think of it in terms of the power the president wields over his political party members in congress, when paradoxically it is this same congress that is supposed to keep the president in check and not the other way around. By design the board of directors, like congress, is made to be a check on the authority of the CEO, but in practice, because of the power of the CEO's stock options and the favorability of the stockholders who only look at profits and typically know next to nothing about what is actually going on in the organization the CEO holds great sway over the board of directors. Thus, a successful CEO, in terms of profits, only checks on their behavior are self-imposed and therefore only limited by their own moral compass.

The theoretical concept of the business model is that you have revenue and expenses. Through hard work revenue exceeds expenses resulting in a profit. Out of that profit investments are made to improve the productivity of the workforce in a perpetual model. What the theory fails to take account of is the human aspirations of the employer. Unlike the employee the employer has the ability to determine what percentage of profits are allocated to his or her salary. Thus, the employer can make choices such as which is better more productivity or purchasing a new fishing boat. The employer, like most human beings, is going to follow the desires of their heart. During the Civil War the Confederacy because they operated under slavery preferred manpower to machines because labor was less expensive. Because the North had to pay their workers' wages, they industrialized to make their workers more efficient. Thus, the more expensive the worker the more the resources are put into them to maximize their output, because as workers get more expensive the less cost technology becomes to enhance each worker's productivity.

Some have argued that raising the minimum wage will take the poor out of poverty. The problem with this logic is that the value of money is equal to production. Raising the minimum wage does not raise the earnings of the workers because the prices will automatically inflate to the production ability within society. For instance, if the minimum wage was $100,000 an hour this does not mean that everyone will suddenly become rich. Rather a cheeseburger will suddenly cost $50,000. Thus, to decrease poverty the efficiency of society must increase. To increase the value of the employee we must increase their efficiency and make it in the employer's best interest to do so. Therefore, we stipulate that the salaries for the CEO's and board of directors may not be greater than 10 times the salary of their least paid employee or 5 times the mean salary of the organization's domestic workforce, whichever is higher. While some on the left have suggested salary caps, such things inadvertently are attempting to put a cap on human potential. Thus, the argument is not to cap the salary, but a realization that the employees were also instrumental in the achievement of the organization, and they should also be carried along for the ride. In America's early history there was a race among railroads to cross the American continent. When the east railway finally linked to the west the CEO came out to give a speech praising himself and management for completing this monumental task. Then the CEO walked over to nail in the last spike, thus completing the line. Swing. Miss! Swing again, hit on the side sending the spike off into the air. After several failures he handed the sledgehammer to other members of management who had similar results. Some did not even have the strength to lift the sledgehammer. Finally, they gave the sledgehammer to one of the men on the line. One hit and done! Consider what kind of corporation would you want to work for, a heartless machine where you are a mindless cog to collect a paycheck, or an organic organism where the life of each piece is viewed as vital to the momentum of the whole?

Now I realize that the term salary is relative. Most employers pay a great deal more for each employee than they received on their paychecks. Such expenses include health insurance, pensions, etc. Then there are the costs associated to each employee, from the tools to do their trade, to the utilities to keep the lights on. The employer also has ways of being rather loose with what constitutes their own wages and what constitutes a legitimate business expense. For instance, do they fly coach, or first class, or take the company jet? Inefficiency at the top does just as much harm to any organization as inefficiency at the bottom. The difference is the top can put controls that force employees under them to spend wisely, but in the absence of government interference the employer is accountable to none, but themselves. The current ratio as of 2024 of worker compensation to that of the CEO is on average 350 times greater in the United States, not including the excesses of business expenses. These are wages and excesses that are not reinvested into new markets, new technologies, or increased production. The employees in the business make it an organic institution. These numbers tell me that the average CEO is not working for the betterment of the organization but themselves. Capitalism in its best form is driven through the needs of the market, which is the people. If the cost to the business for its cheapest employee to perform their duties is X amount, then the amount for the employer should be limited to not exceed 10 times at amount. On each business trip I never ate at the hotel restaurant because the cost for the meal was exorbitant. I pondered why would anyone eat here at these prices? I got the answer on one trip when I came with the boss and management elite, and they all went to the hotel restaurant because it was convenient. I said, hey guys one meal here is triple my daily allowance for food. The restaurant across the street is half the cost for twice the amount of food." Everyone laughed, "Who cares, the company is paying for it." On another occasion I was in the cafeteria line at work waiting to pay for my meal. Many of the people in line with me were foreign workers making minimum wage. One of the executives came in. Cut in line. Ordered his meal. When asked, "How will you be paying?" He responded, "Charge it to the company." Never seen him or any member of management break bread with those under them and here you had the least paying for their meal and those making six and even seven figure salaries were unwilling to even pay for their own lunch.

If you believe me to be placing a cap on salaries, you are reading this incorrectly, rather the gain or decline of the organization should be felt universally, with the greatest gains and declines felt by the executive because they are manning the oar. The purpose of any business should be to satisfy the needs of the public, but in America labor's existence is turned upside-down as the people exist to meet the needs of management. At a certain point American Corporations lost the humanity of their workforce and began to look upon them as part of the machine needed to render a specific output. The realization that the same labor could be achieved overseas at 10 percent of the cost caused America's manufacturing based to migrate to the developing world. Management used multiple cost cutting measures to drastically improve the efficiency of the workers abroad. Over time industrializing those nations. As more corporations migrated overseas the demand for the workers increased. This demand over time forced wages up such that in 1980 the pay for a worker in China was 50 cents an hour, but by 2018 it was $5.50. At a certain point many of the workers realized they could make the transition from employee to employer. Because they knew the skills and could achieve a significantly higher pay than a worker's salary but was still significantly lower than their American CEO counterpart. Thus, they could sell their products at a competitive advantage because the pay for management was so drastically reduced. The American Corporations failed, and their Chinese counterparts succeeded. American Corporations only considered the waste and inefficiency at the bottom as important because America stressed individualism which idolized CEOs such as Elon Musk, Bill Gates, and Jeff Bezos as supermen. While the Chinese through Communism stressed the importance of the community. Thus, their Chinese equivalents viewed the corporation as a whole and themselves as a part of that whole. They considered the waste and inefficiency at both the top and the bottom as vital to the wellbeing of the company and placed themselves subservient to the needs of the business.

Racism and bigotry also played their part. American management simply felt more at home in America. They felt a bond to their culture, language, etc. This increased the gulf between management and the employees as management increasingly distanced themselves from their own workforce. The ever-widening gap in wages also further eroded any since of equality between the two groups. As the wages grew overseas the third world began to transform into the developing world as the public in these foreign marketplaces became further able to purchase the same products, they were manufacturing. Because the third world was now manufacturing the technology, the technology itself became less and less of a mystery to the general population which spurred further entrepreneurship in the marketplace even beyond the technology available in the United States. Correspondingly as the manufacturing base was outsourced the wages of the United States began to stagnant and the technology knowledge base among the general population began to erode. Because the top of the chain was making huge profits overseas, they used these profits to erode anti-monopoly and other governmental organizations that put any restrictions on their behavior and even used legislation to compel the government to purchase their products at exorbitant prices, especially in the healthcare field. Soon it became apparent that rigging the system in each company's interest was less expensive to turn a profit than investing in technology which was becoming exponentially more expensive as the factories and technological centers of the United States had been long ago exported out of the country. Conversely like the Confederacy because the domestic labor pool was becoming cheaper than investing in technology US companies began to de-evolve back to manual labor when available. As the workforce became more expendable rather than put trust and faith in their people their employees were seen as suspect and something to be guarded against which furthered internal bureaucracy and decreased efficiency. Originally taking advantage of cheap labor overseas lowered the price of consumer goods, but as the wages stagnated the buying power of the US consumer dropped. As the wealth poured back into the top one percent, they built bigger homes and other things which required a more domestic labor force transforming the public into indentured servants in one form or another.

If US Corporations had poured their profits into research and development, technology, etc. rather than themselves the US would still demand a leading edge in the world, but rather than technology they used their money through manipulation to attempt to rig the US to their advantage. It was only a matter of time before they utilized the powers of the US government to attempt to manipulate the world to their advantage. However, in industrializing the third world, the third world was also developing the ability to fight back. Thus, the emergence of BRICS and the decline of American hegemony.

The argument is often raised that as efficiency increases the workforce for any organization shrinks. This as a net positive. Once again consider China, as efficiency expanded labor became increasingly available for new industries and technologies. When tying the pay of the lowest paid workers to the highest paid worker, the CEO, consider the lowest paid workers are typically jobs anyone can do. The custodial staff for instance, installs the toilet paper and paper towels in the restrooms, yet if the company had installed bidets and air-driers such tasks would not be needed. Is not the value of such people provided purely for our convenience of greater value to humanity? Does your job maximize your potential or is your potential yet unrealized?

PRIVATIZATION OF GOVERNMENT

My belief is that for nearly all of us it is the latter. My goal may seem counter-intuitive, but once a society is achieved where all manual labor is automated humanity can be transformed from that of manual labor into a society of scientists, artists, and philosophers. Others say, aren't you worried about robotics and artificial intelligence taking over all the jobs? If it liberates humanity beyond the paradigm of labor through compulsion, then I am all for it.

The real travesty in society is how very few live up to their potential. We live in a world that compels us to work for the dreams of others when our goal should be to utilize the human spirit to compel each of us to pursue our own dreams. Where the curiosity of the mind to solve all the riddles, be they nature, the universe, ourselves, and/or society drive humanity beyond the limitations that we impose upon ourselves. This book is a testament to the possible fruits of such an endeavor. Yet today the distribution of capital often misses society's would be greatest entrepreneurs. There is a bridge we need to cross to arrive at that destination between the world of our dreams where we can follow where our human spirit takes us, and the existing world that compels us to forced servitude so that we may have bread.

So the question follows what about the people that fall through the cracks? Remember from the previous section there are no state governments. I transcended the state government system to the halos. Each halo modelled after a department of the Federal Government. One department for hospitals and medicine, another to combat poverty, another for higher education, another for those suffering from mental disease etc. Consider there are many professions that are not motivated by financial gain. What motivates the missionary? What motivates the person working at the food bank? These organizations have been designed around the concept of the Peace Corps. They are voluntary positions, yet they will cure diseases, and get people out of poverty. The biggest cost in any organization is the pay for the workers. Because these are voluntary positions, they can absorb large portions of the unemployed population providing a socialist economic competitor to the capitalist. Because the motivation of these halos is not capitalist economics, which is based on raising the standard of living for the individual, but socialist economics, which is based on raising the standard of living for the community. Thus, socialism through the public sector is put into competition with the private sector for labor. Because the government model is a direct democracy, not a republic, the people themselves will be able to reform one side or the other. And of course, the people vote with their feet in so far as to which side they choose to render their labor. Remembering both communism and capitalism had a way of enslaving their population. One could argue that both were running in opposition to the intentions of their founders, yet the devolution of society has a predictable path as power always longs for more power at the expense of the many over the few. A truly democratic government, of, by, and for the people must have authority over the compulsion of any force that attempts the enslavement of society.

I want to make a paradigm shift in how we perceive business. The CEO and board of directors are employees of the corporation and as employees must be held accountable for its well-being. The employer is the customer. Or put another way the employer of any business is the people and thus even the CEO and board of directors should be held accountable to them. Thus, the will of the people is expressed through the direct democracy to enforce their power over their businesses as their employer. Thus, the society functions through capitalism, but that capitalism is at the discretion of the public vote. There is a warning I would present to the people. Just as the people require freedom, the more freedom given to business the greater the innovation they will bring to society, thus is the power of laissez-faire. For this reason, as you will note throughout this section my effort is to unleash, rather than restrain business and entrepreneurship.

Looking back on the American Revolution it is important to understand that the European world at that time operated under a feudal system. Where the gentry under lords held total sway over the surfs. Adam Smith's the Wealth of Nations offered a novel concept which we now reference as capitalism that the surf's could quit their jobs and decide which lord to work under. Also, that inefficient lords could go bankrupt so that only the profitable and efficient lords would remain. To further restrain their power the US Constitution put two checks over the lords. First the people's house where the people could elect leaders to put laws into place that restrained the power of the lords over them. Second, they put into place the Senate to utilize the power of the states over them. With the seventeenth amendment the power of the Senate was neutralized as the state governments lost their voice to the national government. The people's house has also been devolved into a house of lords as each elected member of congress is now a representative, not of the people, but of the corporate aristocracy. As the lords purchased the press, the "free press" devolved into a propaganda machine. In the previous section my effort was to undo their strangle hold over congress through the long overdue transition to a directly democratic government where the people represent themselves. The propaganda machine of the press remains a threat as lobbying will transition from congressional representatives to the public at large. However, when the people become the congress the ability of the corporate aristocracy is greatly restrained and one way or another the truth always comes out.

Little Republics to Little Democracies
In a perfect world advancement at any corporation would be purely and only through merit, but in my experience nepotism, personal friendships, yes men, sycophants, flattery, alcohol, and other nefarious activities all play their part in one's ability to climb the corporate ladder. At the top of the chain corporations function as *Little Republics*. The Board of Directors as the congress of the corporation with the chairman of the board representing the Speaker of the House. This congress is elected through a shareholder vote, notably absent in this vote is the employees of the corporation. Each vote in this instance is not equitable as those with more shares represent a greater share of the vote than others, thus those with more wealth have a greater voice in the election of the board members, just as congressional representatives are subservient to those who "invest" or "bribe" their congressional representatives in the form of campaign contributions. Because the stock holdings of the employees are immaterial in terms of wealth to that of the wealthy, their voice in the board is typically reduced to nonexistence in the vote for the Board of Directors.

PRIVATIZATION OF GOVERNMENT

The Chief Executive Officer, a.k.a. the CEO, functions as the President of the corporation with a cabinet. Each member of the cabinet, like the US President, represents a different department of the corporation. Such as, one member of the cabinet may be the Vice President of Engineering, while another the Vice President of Marketing, etc. And finally, the shareholders function as the voting population.

In the previous section I disclosed the failures of the republican form of government in the public sector, specifically the national congress. It is important to acknowledge, because the same *little republics* also exist in the private sector in the form of corporations the same failures exist as it does in the national congress because they were constructed using the same framework and ideology. Yet in some instances it is even worse, because all citizens of age and in good standing with the law can vote for their representatives, but only the shareholders are citizens of a corporation, because only the shareholders have a voice in the election of the board of directors, while the employees without shares are as *illegal aliens* without a democratic voice. Beyond that, the president of a country is elected by its citizens, but the CEO and his cabinet are also not elected by the employees, even though the employees are their subjects as the relationship between a lord and a serf and a master and a slave.

To combat this labor unions formed to represent the workers. For a time, this worked, but like all powerful positions it too was abused. Laws forced workers to pay into the unions. Many unions spanned multiple industries and had the ability to wield labor like a weapon. Such formed the New York mafia to force many corporations to provide lucrative positions for the Don's family that only existed on paper. This breakdown occurred because the union existed as a third-party force to the business enterprise. Also, while the union's purpose is to increase wages and benefits, which it is successful at, it often divorces itself from the productivity, efficiency, and technological needs of the organization. A business cannot divorce itself from such needs and stay solvent in the long run. Rather my goal is to transform the corporation from a model under a republic to that of a democracy in line with our democratic goals and to do so through a method that amplifies merit, efficiency, productivity, and growth that will in turn justify higher wages and benefits. Understandably the labor unions were born out of desperation as a counterweight to management, but both the extortion of the labor union to arbitrarily force wages up, and the excesses of management to force wages down are equally wrong because both utilize force a.k.a. authoritarianism to achieve their ends. Rather to be democratic and equitable from labor's side the work must justify the pay rendered and from management's side the pay must be reasonable for the work rendered. To achieve such a utopian state of business delves into a much deeper issue.

The founders of the United States Constitution preferred a republic over a democracy, citing that only a republic, rather than a democracy, would preserve the rights of the minority over the will of the majority. The minority they were referencing was the wealthy aristocracy and the majority they were referencing was the poor. Because in a republic only the wealthy can afford to run for congress, they knew that despite the party in power the members of congress as the corporate aristocracy would defend their capital from the poor majority. Whereas in a government where the people themselves are given the authority, such as through a direct democracy, the people through their power could forcibly re-distribute the wealth as took place during Shay's rebellion. Their argument was that the poor only work through compulsion. If the rich are taken out of the equation no one would work, and production would grind to a halt. Such was the premise of Ayn Rand's best seller, Atlas Shrugged. The evils of capitalism are abundant, but with all its evils it remains among the most productive of all the economic systems. Thus, the gravity of the dilemma becomes clear. How do you introduce freedom, democracy, and entrepreneurship into an economic system that relies on compulsion and fear to maximize production without the whole system imploding?

American Individualism plays to the vanities of leadership, be it in business, the media, or politics, using their ego to believe that their direction is better than anyone else's within their organization and as one exalts themselves, they often miss the best talent right under their nose. I have discovered that people will work infinitely harder to fulfill their own ideas over the ideas of others. Google developed the "20% time" where the employees are allowed to dedicate twenty percent of their working hours to what they think will most benefit the corporation. This provided the employees a method to vote through their labor on the technological path of the company. Among the advances that came out of this was the Android OS. There is also something to be said that the best employees aren't the ones you hire, they are the ones you create. For this reason, I would like to advance the *Employee-Owned Company* as an evolving alternative in the workplace. The Board of Directors is elected by the shareholders, but if the employees are the majority of shareholders, they have a direct voice in who their CEO is and if that CEO is allowed to retain their position. For most portions of the organization the CEO should be empowered to determine their cabinet, because in this way when things go wrong the CEO cannot shift blame but is legitimately held accountable. Yet there are positions beyond the CEO that should be reserved and hired through the Board of Directors, such as the Controller a.k.a. the chief accountant. This would allow the board to retain direct control over the purse strings of the organization to keep the CEO in check. Beyond that unlike the other positions in the company the head of Human Resources should be elected and retain their position through the will of the employees via an election where each employee may cast a single anonymous vote. As among the purposes of HR is to voice the complaints of the employees, he should thus be directly accountable to them with a seat on the board of directors as a representative of the employees to ensure the legality and legitimacy of the corporation. In an open environment there should be nothing that human resources can tell the board that management doesn't already know. Also reporting directly to the board of directors means that his or her job is not put in jeopardy when revealing any malfeasance of management.

Beyond that, just as we offered shires/counties the right to put proposals on the ballot, once a corporation reaches a specific size the employees should be able to submit proposals to amend the company's corporate bylaws. Of course, those bylaws are subordinate to the laws passed through public vote, be they local or federal. Just like any law passed, whether it is through the people or otherwise, some will lead to success and others will lead to ruin. The employees will endure the fate of their own choices. In this way the employees will mold their corporate world. As we alluded too previously, I have also created a socialist world, which I will discuss in the next section, so that each citizen can follow the proclivity of their heart and bring the learning of the one world into that of the other.

It is true that corporations set up their own bylaws, but there are also significant public laws that govern corporations. There are several reasons companies are forced to convert from privately held companies to corporations. First the tax code is written in such a way that the tax burden on small business owners becomes extreme once they reach a specific profit margin, while the tax burden on corporations is significantly lower. Second as a company moves from a privately held company to a publicly held company the potential for a large degree of capital to flow into the company through the acquisition of public stock. Third, power is difficult to relinquish, but the formation of a corporation dictates the creation of a board of directors, which offsets the power of the CEO, allowing wisdom from other successful corporations through independent board members to flow into the business. Often the original owner, because he doesn't want to relinquish any power will attempt to fill the board with close personal friends and relatives. If the board is going to serve its purpose the investors must be allowed to have their say thus independent investors must have a seat or multiple seats on the board of directors.

Beyond these arguments for a publicly held company, the startup costs for most businesses can be extreme. It is difficult to move forward when you are sitting on a mountain of debt. As a company goes public their hope is that the company will get an incursion of capital to offset their debts as well as capital to innovate and expand the organization. The largest investors were typically current or former business owners themselves and bring with them their wisdom through the board of directors.

There are also multiple downsides to public ownership. The price to earnings ratio also known as the P/E ratio is one method of determining if the value of the stock price is reasonable or overvalued. Public perception pays a large part in the growth of some stocks over others. Technological advancements can create excitement in the marketplace leading to a massive surge in buying this stock or that. As investors see a stock price soaring often many will want to jump on the bandwagon in hopes of a quick profit. At a certain point the price of stock out paces the company's earnings. For instance, Nvidia at its peak reached a value of stock that was about 250 times the value of its earnings. At a certain point as the price of stock significantly out paces the corporation's earnings a bubble begins to form in the industry and the bigger the bubble gets the greater the chances that the bubble will pop. Whether it was the dotcom bubble or the Artificial Intelligence bubble, when these bubbles crash, they threaten to take down the economy with them. Public ownership is great for startup corporations because it creates a boost for up-and-coming technologies in the marketplace, but as businesses reach a certain size the girth of the corporation itself makes it less nimble as upper management becomes further and further removed from the average employee and as such the employee feels a sense of disconnection from the organization. Thus, the smaller corporations through their communication can be infinitely more nimble and productive, because management often works so closely with the employees that each employee feels a part of the organization and their motivation to make the corporation succeed goes beyond pay and benefits. The challenge is how to achieve among the employee base of a large corporation the same feeling of belonging and voice that an employee has at a small corporation. Thus, an argument can be made that the need of public funds no longer exists after a company reaches a certain size and as such the businesses success or failure should ride on its own merits through the voice of its employees to meet the demands of the marketplace without the incursion of public shareholders. My solution goes beyond the life cycle of businesses. Rather an evolution of the business model so that rather than die of old age the minds and creativity of their employees can make the corporation an immortal entity perpetually evolving to ever greater heights.

This is my recommendation. In all cases the allocation of company stock shall be equal between board, employee, and management both foreign and domestic in proportion to their income. Of course, foreign stock allocations are subjected to the constraints of foreign and international laws. The formation of each corporation is followed by three "winds" each to take place at the discretion of management. The first wind will begin when the corporation goes public. The second wind will begin when the employees are able to amend the corporate bylaws through a shareholder vote. The third and final wind will begin when the corporate bylaws can be amended through a vote of one employee, one vote. Stock may not be sold publicly if the P/E ratio surpasses 25, the employee ownership is less than 4% of the total shares held times the numbers of years passed the adoption of each wind. The shares held by the Board, the CEO, and his executive cabinet are not to be considered part of the employee shares. The Board, the CEO, and his cabinet are not required to relinquish any existing shares owned, however they may not purchase new shares if the number of shares owned is collectively greater than 100% of the shares held for the first wind, 50% of the second wind, and 25% of the third wind minus 4% of the total shares held each successive year following the beginning of each wind. After freedoms of each wind are granted, they may not be undone by management. If a company merges or acquires or is acquired by another domestic company the greatest wind level shall exist to all employees' company wide. If a corporation of the kingdom acquires a foreign public company the first wind transition for all branches of the corporation within that foreign nations shall begin. Shares earned by the employee as an employee foreign or domestic shall be considered part of the employee share percentage, despite layoff, resignation, termination, or retirement until death or sale. Upon death remaining shares shall pass to a beneficiary as designated by the employee. Shares held by beneficiaries shall be counted against the public shares.

Thus, corporations in our new system of government shall perpetually transition from management and the public to the employees. Each *wind* represents a greater relinquishment of the powers of management and a greater enhancement of the powers of the employees. At a certain point, provided the continuance of the corporation, the employees alone will be able to earn corporate shares, while management will be accountable to the employees and the marketplace. In this way new corporations get the capital they need to get off the ground and through a gradual shift each corporation migrates from public to employee ownership. Once it becomes totally employee owned, or at least nearly so, the company will have aged. It will be up to the employees to keep the corporation on a technological edge. These are dangerous times for the company. Younger companies will be getting the lion's share of investment capital. Thus, older businesses that do not stay current will not artificially continue on life-support through the flow of public capital. Allowing corporations to die from aging technology is just as important as giving them life for new technology. Working for small companies each employee feels the loss and gain of each dollar, but the bigger the corporation, the greatest the general feeling of, "Who cares the company is paying for it!" I make it more difficult for larger corporations because I know they are going to have a built-in advantage and I don't want them to stagnant but become equal to the work of their hands.

As entrepreneurs form corporations around new technology the price to earnings ratio expands investors' enthusiasm. However, as more shares are allocated to the employees and away from the public and management the P/E ratio will naturally drop giving earnings a chance to catch up with the price per share. Having a cap on the P/E ratio curbs the threat of bubbles forming in the industry. In this way the stock market will become less of a casino and migrate toward merit-based growth. At the beginning of each wind as long as the corporation can grow their earnings judiciously to keep up with the P/E ratio, technically there will be no cap on public investment as an incentive for workers and management alike to advance and grow the business. As corporations transition from publicly owned to employee owned the focus is moved from profit through share price to the real profits achieved through production. Beyond that the members of the board are no longer novices, but experienced business leaders, which may consider investing in smaller companies and joining their boards to pass along their wisdom. Thus, just as humanity evolved from a monarch to a republic, to a direct democracy, each of the best corporations will also evolve from a single owner business (a monarchy) to a board (a republic), to a completely employee-owned corporation (a democracy), to an employee run organization (a direct democracy). In time this too will evolve.

My prayer is that through corporate expansion into foreign markets the realization of the shift from publicly owned corporations to employee-owned corporations' will become internationally realized and championed. Through this economic transition the reputation of the kingdom will follow as a government model that represents the people in concrete terms rather than mere propaganda. I offset this against the United States which has presented itself as the pinnacle of capitalism and democracy. Through globalism it built factories around the globe. Through the avenue of cheap labor corporate profit skyrocketed exponentially expanding corporate influence in Washington, which increasingly became a tool of corporations to exploit the developing world through its people and its resources. Those governments that would not comply were overturned through the CIA, congressional sanctions, or the threat of military force. Yet as the world conformed to capitalism through the heavy hand of the United States their corporations began to compete over cheap foreign labor. Competition, the principal element of capitalism in practice, forced wages to rise. The factories that the US built began to create the rise of a middle class in these nations and the power of those nations followed suit. But as these nations came of age and America's own manufacturing capacity plummeted the buying power and wages of the American and European citizens fell. Conversely, as the developing world rose through capitalism the perversion of the truth became self-evident that American corporations had no desire for these nations to pull themselves out of poverty, but rather desired them to be eternally impoverished and reliant upon the United States. America's calls for democracy and capitalism were in reality a demand for tyranny and slavery. Thus, a global stain on capitalism has been created and if capitalism is going to make a legitimate resurgence it must evolve to a state where the rhetoric conforms to reality so that it is seen and felt encouraging both market expansion and true democratic values.

It is important to note, just because the people are given a direct-democracy government model does not mean that the people will use that government model to make the right decisions. Democracy in the private sector carries the same warning. The difference being the people will be accountable for the decisions that they make, rather than those foisted upon them through which they had no say, which is the present model. Case in point, at United Airlines the workers union passed and forced a resolution that flight attendants were not to assist passengers with their luggage. This rule was particularly difficult on their elderly passengers who were forced to turn to other passengers to look for assistance. Anytime the needs of the customers are considered less than the desires of the employees' customers will take offence and will do their business elsewhere. Remember our paradigm shift, the customer, as in the people are the boss. The only rule I have in business is do unto others as you would have others do to you. Work is work. If it wasn't work, they would call it playtime. It is human nature to want to rest, to resist labor and to make it lighter. Solomon said it this way, *"A little sleep, a little slumber, a little folding of the hands to rest, and poverty will come upon you like a robber, and want like an armed man."* When it comes to the private sector the controlling hand of the government to restrict the toil of a man from his labor, must be removed to the greatest extent possible, because to do otherwise removes the flexibility of the human spirit through laissez-faire to let the market evolve itself. The private sector is dynamic, where changes made are refined, and refined again. Through success and failure give the private sector the task and then let the people through the direct democracy refine and tweak it. It is difficult for those in power to relinquish that power, even when it is for their own benefit. Flattery exalts the ego to gain confidence and manipulation follows, but love speaks the truth. Thus, I began my section for the capitalist with a true reflection of what can become of it if used in the wrong ways and for the wrong reasons. Just as a reckoning came to eastern communism, a greater reckoning is coming to western capitalism. In the interim, that capitalism may live beyond this coming upheaval against it, I present these suggestions of which their success or failure time will be the judge.

The pyramids of corporations are not so dissimilar to those of government structures, though the inequality is not wealth, but power and to these I will combat with the force of law. Their remains a great difficulty to creating a merit-based system of government. A privatization of the government that does not descend into a feudal system. With rare exceptions all elected officials from congress to governors, to even local mayors, all arrive at their position from the top 1% of income earners. This is not necessarily a bad thing as previous heads of organizations bring with them leadership skills which are necessary to run cities and federal departments. Though there also exist dangers, such as corporate lobbyists in America are routinely put in charge of the same regulating agencies over their behavior. It is for this reason that in my new system of government department heads are now elected, rather than appointed positions. In the United States leadership terms such as Mayor, CEO, President were adopted to separate themselves from the equivalent feudalist European terms, lord, baron, etc. Among the primary differences between capitalism and feudalism is the religious aspect of feudalism, in that the lord and monarch have a divine obligation before God to look after the people within his sphere of influence, whereas because the serfs can change lords in capitalism there is a dispassionate separation between management and their employees. As capitalism holds to the view that through the paycheck rendered an employer's obligation to their employee has been financially satisfied. Thus, I am going to use the terms of a feudal system, not because I believe any human being is superior to that of another, but to re-establish the divine responsibility the lord has to his serfs under his charge. It is also in part to remind the people of their origins from which their system comes from. Americans have long touted the freedom of their society, yet American civilization as all civilizations that came before it since the dawn of civilization have been ruled by money and power. In the words of Daniel Webster, "There are men of all ages who mean to govern well, but they mean to govern. They promise to be good masters, but they mean to be masters." The effort of enlightenment is to acknowledge the reality of humanity and then use that reality to bring out the best within the human spirit, rather than to fight in opposition to it. In the face of "might makes right," carry the torch toward the most prophetic profound delusion of all, the meek shall inherit the earth."

Strengths and Weaknesses of People vs. Ideas

Among the paradoxes of democracy is the concept of leadership, as democracy looks to the many, but leadership looks to the one. The draw of democracy is that everyone wants to be heard. To feel and believe that our voice matters. The draw of capitalism is that everyone also wants to be the hero, the victor, the champion. It is the vanity of leadership that creates the necessity of democracy, but it is the abhorrence of mediocrity which compels the capitalist. In the previous section, I established the foundational building stones of the law-creation process to bring a voice to the voiceless. However, merely creating a law serves no purpose unless the government can provide the means of enforcement. And enforcement by its nature empowers the enforcer. As the power of the enforcer is increased, be it management, police, military, the liberties, and voice of the people are correspondingly diminished. As the power of the enforcer diminishes the anarchy of the citizens, employees, etc. increase. The authority is perpetually looking for structure and order, while the people are seeking liberty and representation. Fear of disorder and chaos leads management and governments to curtail liberties, which is a denial of failure to teach its lessons. This is the failure of government over business because governments have been denied the ability to fail. Consider as I put forward a new model for corporations, that in the end as it is run by the people, I am not ambivalent to the fact that many of these corporations will go under. Like all new industries in the beginning more will fail than will succeed, but in each failure, there are lessons learned. There is a sad reality to our nature as human beings. Words are not always enough. Some lessons are only learned through the consequences of our actions. In the Old Testament the prophets would tell the people the right way, but their words were ignored, disregarded, mocked, and trivialized. Ultimately, just as the modern-day prophets such as, Abraham Lincoln, Martin Luther King, Jr. Malcom X, most paid the ultimate price for speaking truth. Repeatedly Israel had to experience subjugation millennia after millennia before they were ready to adhere to the message of the final prophet. Everyone believes they can do things better than everyone else, but once you are in the ring it is an entirely different matter. Imagine if local governments competed like businesses where they were allowed to try new things and when and if they failed, they could do so in a way that the whole economy and government system remained running. Allowing the cream to rise to the top so that the best is emulated in a continual process of improvement and competition. In the words of Theodore Roosevelt, *"It is not the critic who counts; not the man who points out how the strong man stumbles, or where the doer of deeds could have done them better. The credit belongs to the man who is actually in the arena, whose face is marred by dust and sweat and blood; who strives valiantly; who errs, who comes short again and again, because there is no effort without error and shortcoming; but who does actually strive to do the deeds; who knows great enthusiasms, the great devotions; who spends himself in a worthy cause; who at the best knows in the end the triumph of high achievement, and who at the worst, if he fails, at least fails while daring greatly, so that his place shall never be with those cold and timid souls who neither know victory nor defeat."*

To bring about such an evolved form of local government requires a complete reformation of local government as we know it. It also requires the empowerment of leadership to draw in the fighters, those with the most creative and dynamic solutions. Those courageous souls who challenge the odds to try new things as takes place every day in the free market. In China they ranked the GDP growth of each city so that local governments were put into a place of competition for who could increase the output of their city the most. The result was the fastest growing nation in the world. Yet unlike China I must create natural competition among local governments in a manner that also aligns with my democratic goals. Government does not run only on Election Day. Funds are required to pay for the roads we drive on, for example, aqueducts that provide us with water, and hydroelectric dams that provide our homes and businesses with daily energy. For the people, constantly to monitor these internal governmental functions and services would not be practical, but a truly democratic society can exist only if the people of that society have control over which services its government provides and how much they will be taxed for them. Some positions in government require oversight in one way or another by officials of the government. The best method, as is the Prince of the Covenant, is to have those officials appointed by God, as only <u>Love</u> knows their heart, unfortunately, in the present we do not always have this luxury available to us. Yet the foundation building blocks of Jezreel (Direct

PRIVATIZATION OF GOVERNMENT

Democracy) must be assembled in such a way that they make these elected officials and nobility directly accountable to all the people.

My task then is to devise solutions for each of these issues that, if managed wrongly, could diminish the representation of the cast-aside man, and at the same time, a unified system of government is maintained. To add further complexity to the situation, any solution must establish a political environment that allows the people themselves to write their own destiny without gradual loss to representation or paving a road to disunity between the units of government, with the result of some form of internal discord.

This section explains the infrastructure of each level of our Kingdom of Heaven.[1] First, to properly understand this section, it is necessary to differentiate the naming differences between a *kingdom* and a *nation*. For only in a kingdom would you have dukes, knights, mages (magicians), a wizard, a court jester, etc. Second, with such a title, *the Kingdom of Heaven*, in and of itself is a land of myth and legend, therefore for a true realization from legend to reality, we are going to need to use a little bit of magic and draw upon the myths and legends of humanity's past. We will begin, therefore with a general understanding of terms regarding this infrastructure. The *kingdom*, not nation, is divided into ten *realms,* not states as the borders of the realm are ideological in nature and not physical. The realms are divided into *shires*, not counties. The physical division is into *shires*, (known in the United States as counties). The shires are further separated into cities, towns, villages, etc. The head of each realm in a heavenly kingdom is a *shepherd*[2], as they are divided ideologically, not a governor which is divided by a land mass, and the head of each city is a *lord* if they are male or a *lady* if they are female, (in the USA one may be more familiar with the term mayor). The Shire is governed by the *Shire Fellowship,* not the City Council. Good so far? We will also be introducing a new position called the *Guardian*. The Guardian position is designed around the concept of the labor union and the use of collective bargaining. Only, in this case, the shepherd is filling the role of management, the lords are the labor, and the Guardian is their collective bargainer on their behalf, but more on all this later.

Not forgetting this section has been dedicated to the capitalist a large portion of this domestic infrastructure has been designed around how taxation and government funding may be established democratically, through democratic means. It will also discuss many of society's greatest economic threats, from unemployment to economic recessions and even depressions. Nevertheless, in all instances you will notice that the foundations of this government are designed to defend, preserve, and expand the rights of the people, thus also building upon our humanist agenda from the previous section.

You may notice that the governments of the United States, California, and other states of the U.S.A. are often used as our illustrative examples. This is because learning is based on personal experience and history, I was born in California, and I have lived most of my life in California (and the United States), and the American

---

[1] Hebrews 11:10.

[2] 2 Samuel 24:17; 1 Chronicles 11:2; 17:6, Numbers 17:1-3, etc.

system of government is what I understand best.³ However, because this new system of government is a kingdom, rather than a nation, the English Royal system, nobility, etc. was used as a basis for study due to its stability and integrity as viewed abroad. Also, as English is my primary and only known language, these governments had the greatest wealth of resources for investigation and learning available to me. Had I been born abroad, in Germany, India, or elsewhere, my frame of reference would no doubt have been otherwise. Before we attempt to improve theoretically upon the structure of the present system found in the United States and the United Kingdom, let us analyze the republic form of government in terms of the structure of our local towns and cities. For example, I know that each town is represented by some sort of city court system. I know also that each town government is under the authority of a mayor, or in a kingdom a lord, and a city council, and it usually has several other elected positions, such as judges, district attorneys, and others, depending on the relevant city and state laws. We know that each of the city's elected members represents some different power. This is done, as one might expect, so that each elected official may be counterbalanced by another. By requiring a majority vote from the city council to pass a local city budget, it is hoped to prevent one member of the council from having the sole power to pass a budget that could reflect only his or her own personal interests, or the interests of only his own constituents rather than according to the broader needs of the whole community. A possible problem about this is that by having multiple people involved the creation of the city's budget, this may allow one or two council members, who were in the minority, to blame the others when something goes wrong, and thereby in some cases to avoid their official responsibilities. In addition, the more elected positions there are, the less attention each one gets from the voters on Election Day. Think about it this way: In the last election did the city water inspector whom you most likely voted for do a good job? What about the city assessor or the chief city animal control officer (i.e., the head dog catcher)? How many of them did you really research, to see if they did good jobs? Be honest. How much research about these kinds of elected officials did the electorate really do? How many of your elected city officials could most people even name? What about the judges? How many people really have a good idea about what sort of job—usually—they do? The election of politicians is only as good as the knowledge their societies have about them, but if we reduced the number of elected positions, what would we use as checks and balances to keep them from abusing the system?

If the goal of a government system is to maximize representation of the common person, we need to ask ourselves how much representation the people get from people they elected—but about whom, on the average, they scarcely know anything. Nevertheless, the public cannot be forced to study for an election to do their political homework. To do so would violate their personal freedoms, which would also undermine the very nature of our democratic goals. While the public cannot be forced to study and know the candidates, the election process can be more narrowly focused by decreasing the number of positions on the ballot that are at any one-time up for election. The problem is, of course, that this must be done in a manner that

---

³ Zerubbabel means the one sown of Babylon; referring to a child conceived and born in Babylon

retains the checks and balances over the elected politicians' level of authority, and maintains significant accountability over their behavior. In the present republic system, the city council is needed for the checks and balances to oversee the city's budget.

Given the existing strengths of the republic model for local government, should the lawmaking body of our direct-democracy be made up of elected positions or direct propositions? Direct propositions, while they are the most direct form of representation, lack the ability to run the day-to-day business of the government establishment. For example, the fire department, police department, schools, and libraries—all of them need some person in authority to make sure that budgets are not exceeded, and that the employees within them are all doing their jobs as well as possible, or at least as well as we might reasonably expect. In general, without someone to ensure enforcement of the existing laws that govern the departments of any city, town, or village, the lawmaking process itself would serve no purpose. On the other hand, elected citizens' lack the clarity of written law. When the voters elect a candidate, the chances are that they have only some foggy notions about what the politicians are contemplating, whereas with a law, proposition, or proposal the voter may choose to read everything, right down to the minutest detail in fine print, to understand everything totally. *People,* on the other hand, all too often have less than perfect motives, or they even had bad motives, which they may be reluctant to speak about while they are out on the stump, campaigning for votes, or it may slowly dawn upon us during a political campaign that at times that language may also be used to *not* communicate, to obfuscate, or to be intentionally misleading. In addition, ideas, in the form of written laws, are not subject to bribery in the ways that elected politicians are. Once again, then, we have an ironic twist: We need the day-to-day authority of an elected government position without the power to create laws, and we need representation through propositions that can remain efficiently operational through all the ups and downs of the daily grind of routine business but can also somehow not become gradually degraded or perverted in the process.

Economics of City Government

To accomplish this, we must first look at the county government of our present system to analyze its existing strengths and weaknesses. Recall a shire in the United States is known as a county or township and is nothing more than an area of land made up of towns, less-inhabited areas, and sometimes major cities. If laws are to be enacted through the proposition system, do we do so on a city or a shire level? Right away, various contingencies and considerations pop up, demanding our attention. If laws are enacted on a city level, what is lost is the bond that law would have on a shire level to unite the cities and towns. However, if the shire passes laws, what is lost in that process is the ability of each lord to study closely and then improve upon the financial situation or condition of his or her city. Therefore, we must draw a line between the financial entities and the law-creation process, for in this way they may be analyzed on their own merits, each one, separately.

To help deal with these issues, we can leave the financial decisions and the enforcement of those decisions up to each individual city lord, whereas the creation of law should be done on a shire level, through the propositions, which is better for uniting the towns and cities. Thus, we draw a line between financial decisions and the creation of law. However, obviously, the financial decisions that run a city or a town are important. These decisions affect where the average citizen's personal finances go within his or her own local government. To deprive any person of this right would amount to a huge loss in representation. Remember from America's Declaration of Independence, one of the primary reasons for dissolving their union with Great Britain was, "For imposing taxes on us without our consent."

If the lord, prior to the vote, was to put a tax rate on the ballot and make his or her budget freely available to all on the Web, then the responsibilities of the city council would move directly to the people, for the people would then themselves be approving the budget rather than passing that responsibility off to the city council. This one system improvement has several major benefits over the existing city council system, wherein the people of the city are not given a budget and a tax rate until after the votes are counted. In the present system, this means that a lord may run on lowering taxes or improving services, but then, after the election, his determination and his moral character are the prime movers behind the fulfillment of those campaign promises. Now, however, the people of the city have already the power to see what they would be getting from a candidate, even before the election. This better plan gives the candidates for town or city lord an embedded financial risk and added responsibilities in their budget proposal preparation, and this, in turn, increases the likelihood that the lordship candidates will more carefully study their proposed tax rates and budgets, as they should, *before the election.* This better plan also amplifies the citizens' representation in their government by making the tax rate and budget obligations a choice, rather than subsequently having them foisted upon an only partially knowing population, as is now the case. However, this proposed solution has several difficulties about it that must be overcome.

What can a town do when it runs out of money? If the town goes bankrupt and the lord has the power to increase taxes, then the whole process of voting for a tax rate has been nullified. If a lord can borrow money, then he or she probably forces the problem onto the next lord, and by this roundabout route, the town's financial management system may become a perpetual borrowing plan. This is not as unrealistic as it might seem. The most obvious example of this—on a much larger scale—is the U.S. Congress, which in our time perpetually spends more funds than it takes in every year. Yet we know that economies change. Cities and towns may have major industries suddenly go bankrupt, or they may run into some huge natural disaster for which, to cope adequately, their funds are simply not enough. What, then, can they do?

One option is to require each candidate to plan a contingency surplus. Then if the lord exceeded the allotted budget, there would be up to an additional forty percent available. There are several good reasons for requiring lords to have a surplus, which we will be addressing shortly. Unfortunately, there are also several relevant issues. About this, we need to understand what most people are like. Most of us—including me—like to spend money, but it is saving that is a challenge. Yet what we like to do, and what is best for us to do as human-beings, is not always the same. By having the lordship candidates put their proposed tax rates on the ballot, most of us will be motivated to vote for the lord listing the smallest tax rate because we have other places where we would much rather spend our money. On the other hand, we want our cities to look clean and neat, and to be orderly. For every dollar we donate to taxes, we expect the finest roads and in everything the best possible results. However, let us put ourselves into the lord's shoes. If to run for office, a lordship candidate is pressured to lower taxes; we could expect that he or she will simply account the surplus as part of his budget proposal. That is, we can expect the lordship candidate to subtract the surplus amount required from what the projected total needs to be to provide the lowest taxation possible. Lower taxes translate into more votes as an election plan to get into office. For the contingency surplus to mean anything, there must be reasonable constraints upon when it may be used, in what amounts, and for what purposes. Along with these boundaries, enforceable penalties must be spelled out carefully for any lords who happen to exceed these legal boundaries.

For cities that are growing in population due to immigration or for other reasons, there is an expectation that the city will also require more services, such as, police, fire, schools, and libraries, upkeep of streets and bridges, and timely trash removal. This sudden growth—if for some reason, unexpected—may represent a legitimate need at some point to use more than expected funds, and to do so from the surplus. The reverse is also true. A town can be looking at a declining population for any number of reasons, such as the failure of local industry, or poor decisions about where freeway exits will be placed, but typically, it is the result of poor management decisions. For immigration, with people moving in, there are certain underlying causes, among which we shall mention two. The first is internal, the promise of prosperity, with the belief that their life and the lives of their loved ones will be better in some other place, and the second is some overwhelming external force affecting them, such as civil war, persecution, or famine. The core element of democracy is a belief in, and sensitivity towards, the worth of the cast-aside person, a system that recognizes the value of the common person and has faith and confidence in that person's decision-making capabilities. By allowing population growth to substantially increase the funds available to the lords, we induce competition among the local governments for more people, with the idea of elevating the recognition of the average human-being's inherent value. In the present system, wealth is viewed as more of value than the human-beings who produce it. We must also ask ourselves this fundamental question: Is a nation great because of its financial wealth, or because of its freedoms? Putting taxation and spending up to a vote means that local governments will be controlled by the people of those communities, which confer dignity in a political sense upon the people of that democratic society. These institutions should serve their communities and nations because everyone knows that the people themselves are directly and ultimately responsible for approving their own funding. As adults should be anywhere, they can take care of themselves. By making the amount of funding a lord may use contingent upon population growth, the lord gets a motive to want people to move to his city, to further the service the goals of his office. Essentially, this plan rewards lords for good work, just as it punishes them for poor work, and this is in proportion to the relative prosperity of their towns.

Population growth is just one of many elements that may use this reward-and-punishment system. For example, let us say there is a farming community where hundreds of farmworkers earn next to nothing, and the property owner owns all the land and regularly makes a killing. If population growth, however, is the only rewarding element in the equation, then tyranny is intentionally rewarded, which is in direct opposition to the democratic ideals of this book. However, we may also reward lords who increase their served population's percentage of homeownership.

One of the primary elements will always be the power of a lord to attract thriving businesses and to create an environment in which the average citizen may pursue his or her dreams of success in the business arena.[4] There is a place for the creation of jobs in government-funded institutions, but if we really want a government wherein every person has the maximum amount of liberty, then each one must be able to determine his own destiny. Government-funded jobs tend to come from the minds of political officeholders, which may have many noble purposes, such as the building of an aqueduct, a dam, or a convention center, but these ideas generally originate in the minds of only a few people and probably do not express what most workers really want. Rewarding the lord for creating government-funded jobs, whether by the realm or the federal government, rather than in the private sector, has the potential of opening the door to favoritism among local politicians especially, through the political party system. Attracting business and creating avenues for entrepreneurship locally within a city is much more difficult than being handed a contract from a powerful politician in a position of authority in the realm or federal government. The lord's ability to create opportunities within his own community for the people in the lowest classes and to empower them to build on the desires of their hearts through the private sector is admirable and must be rewarded. It may be difficult to understand fully the impact that simple economics has on liberty every day and in the most practical ways. The poor and the dispossessed may live in what we picture as a free, democratic society, but how much freedom do these people truly have when they are needy families, no roof overhead, no food on the table, and not a penny in their wallets?

Macroeconomics (Unemployment, Recession, and Depression)

At some point, we need to take a step back and critically assess the whole system. If the economy were a static straight line, then rewarding cities through the office of the lord for employing more of their citizens would be an ultimate good. Unfortunately, economics does not run along straight, parallel lines. Sometimes the economy of the whole nation goes downhill. When this happens, if communities were penalized for decreasing available jobs that would make a bad situation worse. The economy represents the livelihood of the average people. Whenever unemployment

---

[4] Free-competition means freedom from physical force to produce for one's own profit, <capitalism.org/faq/competition.htm>.

goes up, two things are always right around the corner: more poverty and more crime.

Having said that we know, however, from a historical perspective, there are several things countries may do to combat their troubled economies. A city or the nation may lower taxation, which means people will have more money to spend, as it is pumped back into the economy, which in turn raises the demand for goods and services. As the demand for goods and services rises, the need for more employees to meet demand increases the needs of business for more workers. Secondly, the national government may increase government spending by creating jobs within the government, such as in road construction and other infrastructure enhancements for business, commerce, recreation, or cultural purposes. Then there are also the more long-term approaches, such as better or more education to increase people's ability to find jobs in business, to fill positions requiring higher-level technical skills, or in research and development with the latest technology, or with greener, more environmentally-friendly technology. Each of these solutions are important, and it is good to use all of them in some way to develop solutions to the normal, age-old economic challenges that all societies have faced since the dawn of civilization, as well as the newer challenges that may be produced by the technologies themselves, or by the world's expanding population.

Up to this point, we have concentrated only on issues at the local government level, but when we are looking at economic issues of the economy, sometimes we need a broader, overall perspective. For this reason, we turn to consider the national government. One way to do this is to tie national government funding to the unemployment levels. This may at first sound complicated, but in the long run, it turns out to be more practical and simpler than one might imagine. To understand this better, we should consider jurisdictional questions so that the rights of the local governments are preserved.

So far, we have looked at only shire and city government as established on a local level. This is practical because it is most logical and necessary to form a Jezreel style of government first at the bottom, closest to the people, and then move upward. It is also true, of course, that there must be national components to tie the independent towns, cities, and shires together. In the modern republic, national governments do this in several ways. The first way is through commerce, which is to say roads, airports, ports of call, etc. The second way is to take account of the obvious physical needs of people where the needed resources are of benefit to multiple separate communities or shires but not cost-effective for one smaller community to financially support on its own. For example, a shire might need aqueducts, reservoirs, dams, or power plants for irrigation and hydroelectric power. The third way is through federal law enforcement agencies such as the Federal Bureau of Investigation and the U.S. Marshals, which address some of society's most fundamental safety and security needs. Finally, through higher education, such as with colleges, community colleges, vocational schools, and universities, business, technology, and other community needs are met, and nothing succeeds as well as having a well-educated, well-informed electorate.

When unemployment increases, the economy needs to produce more jobs or more suitable jobs. One way to deal with this issue is to tie unemployment rates to the spending of the national government, such that when unemployment rises, educational funding also rises, and spending on the government infrastructure, such as with the funding for maintenance of roads and reservoirs also rises, as well as funding for law enforcement, the court system—including the higher courts, criminal investigation, jails, and prisons. The reverse is also true, for as unemployment falls, the national government needs to downsize by releasing jobs to the private sector, thereby helping to fill the employment needs of the business sector. In this way, savings are increased during the good years, which can help to provide for all the increased needs in the bad years—our Joseph principle[5], all of which amounts to sound, basic macroeconomic planning.

Remember, the lord was given a surplus. This surplus provides for the saving in the good years and for the better funding needed in the bad years. As the unemployment rate increases, the percentage of these cities' surpluses, the shepherds (governors) may, in turn, use increases. This is designed to improve productivity as defined by the normal business cycle. As an economy goes down, employers often find themselves forced to let employees go. This results in a smaller number of people being responsible for a larger workload, and the same principle holds true in the governmental sector. As the national government loses funds, it too is forced to let people go, which leaves fewer people to shoulder more responsibility. With this method, one side of the equation is always shrinking and becoming more efficiently productive, while the other side of the equation is expanding to utilize more fully and expand upon the current technology. By this rule, when the business community goes into a recession, the national government expands, and when the private sector economy booms, the national government contracts. Each is designed to fluctuate according to the needs of the economy at the time.

This is the basic foundational principle of macroeconomics, and it is a structural deviation from the republic form of government. One of the fundamental problems with a republic is that because the source of power is the Congress rather than built-in, such automatic adjustments based on this kind of economic data do not occur. The lawmaking process, which tends to be slow by design, is responsible for altering spending, depending upon the state of the economy. Unfortunately, however, the economy does not wait for Congress to act. Typically, by the time the national government does act, the business community is already moving out of the cycle of recession and on through the normal business cycles, and this tends to act in the reverse of what the economy needs by stimulating job growth in the good times rather than the bad. In the present system, as the business economy declines taxation revenues follow that decline, with the result that both the national and local governments are declining, along with the private sector economy, all of which, working in synch, turns a bad situation into a horrendous one. To make the situation worse still, the institutions of government are rarely put into a position of having to

---

[5] Genesis 41:33-36.

contract because they can increase revenues by raising taxes.[6] For this reason, government institutions tend to interact with the economy poorly, producing overall inefficient management.

If taxation on the people is increased more for the needs of the government as an economy goes downhill when money is scarce, we take a bad situation and make it worse by taking away money from the private sector when it needs it most. This would also be pitting the taxpaying population against the government, producing at-large resentment and animosity.

Instead, for the national government, it is more prudent and practical for tax income to come from a percentage of each of the lordship-required surpluses. Still, by tying the city budget surpluses to national government funding, we also do something else important, for the national government is thereby positioned against the city government, which means that the national government will attempt to get as much as it can from the city government, and the city government will be doing all it can to retain its own funds. This plan has multiple benefits. First, the people are better able to believe that when they vote for a lord's budget and tax rate, the lord will fulfill those financial responsibilities, or, if failing that, he or she will have to deal with the national government. Since the national government receives its funding from the cities, the more of the surplus the city spends, the less funding the national government will receive. This makes it natural for the national government to monitor city spending closely, to increase its own revenue. In the present system in most nations, the national government receives most of its funding from the people directly through income taxes. By contrast, the present income system in the United States, which was enacted originally to fund World War II, has become steadily more problematic as the average citizen's financial resources steadily dwindle to the point of being unable to defend his own rights before the state and national governments. Historically, however, this was not the case, and surprisingly, our new concept is derived from the original United States Constitution. Prior to the passage of the Sixteenth Amendment, sometimes known today as the Income Tax Amendment, the national government functioned from a more indirect taxation method known as *excise taxes*.[7] This means that like the national government we propose that they would receive their funds indirectly from the shire government rather than directly from the people, just as the national government was designed originally to receive its funds from the states rather than directly from the people through income taxes. Direct taxation of the common person was against the original United States Constitution. We can see this in Article 1, Section 2, Clause: *Representative and direct taxes shall be apportioned among the several states, which may be included within this union, according to their respective numbers.*

In those earlier times, to raise or increase national taxes, the federal government had to get more tax money from the states. Since the senators were elected by the state legislature, if a senator voted to tax without the authority of the state, he risked

---

[6] Financing a Government, <importanceofphilosophy.com/Politics_FinancingAGovernment.html>.

[7] Constitutional Issues with Taxation, <originalintent.org/edu/>.

losing re-election. History shows that this system of taxation checks and balances managed to keep taxation low at the national level for more than a century.

The city governments, on the other hand, have ample funds, and the stakes are much higher for both the city and the nation because the volume of resources in dispute may mean many millions or even billions of dollars in revenue. To put this in perspective, in 2006 the city budget for Tualatin, Oregon, was 109 million dollars, and Tualatin is just one of many cities in the Portland metropolitan area.

The Wizard of Oz

As we look at the financial structure of the government, it is equally important to analyze the financial structure of the private sector. Historically, among the greatest complaints against direct-representation must be ranked Daniel Shay's Rebellion, which came about after 1786. During that era, the divide between rich and poor was still extreme, and debtor prisons were still, throughout the colonies, very prominent. In fact, a large portion of society was still comprised of indentured servants. Daniel Shay had fought in the major battles of the revolution. Due to the economic hard times, poor people everywhere throughout the colonies were being forced off their land. Daniel Shay organized an armed revolt against the state on behalf of the poor so they would not lose their land, and upper-class people were afraid. After all, they reasoned, if the poor could overwhelm the wealthy in Massachusetts, it was possible that similar revolts could breakout where they lived, or anywhere. When we read today opinions from the American Revolutionary times stating that, *"democracy is rule by the mob,"* most are referring to this event believing that if it were left unchecked America may follow the way of the French revolution where the entire nobility (the rich) were sent to the guillotine. Among the leading voices against democracy was Alexander Hamilton, who said, *"All communities divide themselves into the few and the many. The first are the rich and the wellborn, the other the mass of the people ... The people are turbulent and changing; they seldom judge or determine right."*[8] He recommended that the U.S. form its own monarchy under Washington as he felt the nation needed strong centralized national power to "check the imprudence of democracy." When the designers of the Constitution were referring to "preserving the rights of the minority," the minority to which they were referring was the wealthy. By creating a republic, many of the founding fathers felt that only the wealthy could afford to run for Congress, and therefore, the rights of the wealthy aristocracy would be preserved. We can see this has come to pass as the 113th Congress had a median net worth over a million dollars, which is significantly higher than the net worth of the average American Citizen. Not to mention the average cost of a congressional campaign is 1.6 million, as of 2012, well beyond the reach of an average American Citizen. Therefore banking, foreclosure, and other financial laws remain the power of the national government in the U.S. Constitution. As you can see from Alexander Hamilton's quotation, he did not have much respect for the common American, and this aristocratic prejudice was still common in the Age of Enlightenment, or the eighteenth century. Thomas Jefferson, our visionary, saw

---

[8] "A Constitution for the Few, Looking Back to the Beginning," by Michael Parenti, The International Endowment for Democracy, <iefd.org/articles/constitution_for_the_few.php>.

PRIVATIZATION OF GOVERNMENT

Shay's Rebellion differently, and speaking about it he said, "I hold it that a little rebellion now and then is a good thing, and as necessary in the political world as storms in the physical."

Jefferson accurately saw that Shay's Rebellion brought light to a necessary social injustice that needed a remedy. As we also consider the Tanakh, the rebellion through which Israel revolted from Judah is not so dissimilar and it was God ordained.[9] On the other side of the equation, this government is not designed to be communist. Therefore, we are faced with a conundrum. Capitalism promotes competition among resources for the maximum good of society, yet the goods that this capitalism provides are not equitably shared among the people, leaving many poor, destitute, and homeless. To do away with the financial markets and banking industry would deprive the human competitive drive to move up and make the most from the least. Capitalism, in sum, provides a reward system that communism could never offer. This consideration, in turn, leads us to the question of how can we have a democratic society without putting in jeopardy the advancing competitive drive to enhance society through our banking and other commonly established financial institutions?

Before we can attempt to answer this question, it is important for us to put into context the commonly established financial institutions and talk about how they have progressively evolved in our present era. When considering the financial well-being of any nation, there remains one financial institution above all others, the Federal Reserve. The Federal Reserve is vital because it is responsible for determining the value of the currency itself. This is done by several means, but most notably through the raising and lowering of interest rates. As is always the case before we move forward with the evolution of an institution, we must first look back at the historical composition of the institution itself. In the current republic system of government, other than in the European Union, each Federal Reserve operates on a nation-by-nation basis. Today the commercial world is evolving into an increasingly global economy. Therefore, when we consider the prospects of international currencies, it seems proper that the Federal Reserve, in keeping pace with the business sector, should also move us toward an international government. To date, the closest such institution available is known as the New Development Bank under BRICS. The New Development Bank, however, is not a bank in the traditional sense of the word, rather made with the purpose of mobilizing resources for infrastructure and sustainable development projects in emerging markets and developing countries. Thus, our goal is to have a global reserve, rather than a Federal Reserve, so that no single nation has the hegemonic power of a reserve currency to exploit its power upon other sovereign nations. Such a transition serves to facilitate and reduce the risks of business development and expansion across international borderlines as part of our effort to produce a truly global economy.

However, if any aspect of government is changed, that can have a negative impact on other parts of the whole government. For those who do not know about the current Federal Reserve in America, it is managed by a group known as the Federal Reserve Board, which is composed of six bank industry appointments, six governors, and a chairperson appointed by the president of the United States. Any international

---

[9] 1 Kings 12:21-23. (RETURN)

global reserve must allow for the sovereign voice of the individual member nations. As a rule, the market does best with limitations set into place by the market itself rather than through governmental agents, such as shepherds (i.e., Governors) or special presidential appointments. These forms of government control also come into contrast with our direct-democracy goal of rule directly by the people. We must also consider that the very composition of this new form of government is no longer compatible with previous Board of Governors approach to the Federal Reserve. By increasing national government funding when unemployment goes up, as according to the Joseph Plan,[10] we also give each shepherd an undesirable incentive to raise unemployment. Of course, we know from the Herbert Hoover administration, and from other presidents, that unemployment is a huge motivating factor in elections, and this factor should greatly outweigh the former to increase the employment needs of the nation. Would an NFL or NBA professional sports team wish to do poorly to capture the next year's first draft choice? That seems like a near analogy. Even still, in the existing Republic system of government because all department heads are appointed by the president, if the president loses the election, they in turn also lose their job. Presidents that preside over an economy with high unemployment, high crime rates, high drug addiction, high homelessness, etc. tend to not get re-elected which gives them an incentive to cook the books. To make the world appear much rosier than things are. For instance, during the Biden administration the President continually came out praising the state of the economy as the best ever, yet all over the country tent cities of homeless families began to crop up. The reality and the picture painted by the administration became ever starker. To correct any issue there must first be an acknowledgment that the issue exists. In this new government model because the pay of the national government increases as things get worse, rather than a propensity to cover up undesirable facts the government has the reverse incentive to seek out the issues in the economy to increase their own funding. It is said the squeaky wheel gets the grease. Because the funding is divided between the shepherds by reporting how bad things really are they are liable to get a greater share of the pie of available funds. Funds must also be justified. Thus, it will be incumbent upon the shepherd not only to report *why* more funds are needed, but to also argue *how* their solution will correct the underlying problem. Beyond that because the shepherds are in competition for funds if a shepherd is cooking the books they have an incentive to investigate to get a greater share of the pie themselves. Among the malfeasance in the present republic is quid quo pro where one department head fears investigating another because they risk uncovering the dirt in their own spreadsheets. It's worse than that, because all the department heads are from the same political party because they are all appointed by the same president. Thus, to uncover dirt in one department risks taking down the heads of all departments, because if dirt in one department causes the president to lose the election, they all go down. Thus, the incentive is not to investigate corruption, but to sweep it under the rug. However, in Jezreel the shepherds will be from multiple competing political parties, thus each

---

[10] Genesis 41:33-36.

party has the incentive to investigate and prosecute their competitors to gain leverage come election time.

To allow the public to make an informed decision come election time over the national government department heads, i.e. the shepherds, the public needs the facts to be accurate. What is the crime rate? What is the homeless rate? What is the inflation rate? What is the unemployment rate? These numbers and others like them, are also vital to not only the national government, but the local governments as well. Thus, to ensure the accuracy of the reporting the local shire and city governments are required to sign-off the figures within their local communities. In the daily drama of our nightly news one party is always trying to take the other to court. Because we are human it is expected that innocent mistakes will occur. Communication between the public, the local governments, and various departments should be encouraged to see where the errors occurred and how future reporting may evolve to avoid further mistakes. Repeated failures should create a spotlight into given areas as it may be a sign of a larger problem. We think of the court system in terms of prosecuting an individual for one crime or another, but the courts in our new system should also be available if the public believes the data coming out of one department or another is misleading, inaccurate, or fabricated. The courts can force reporting changes to be made, rather than prosecute the shepherd. Thus, court decisions will be put on the record and come election time the public can determine if another candidate may be better. Thus, local governments and the public are another check on the powers of the department heads that did not exist in pre-existing republics and as the reporting is enhanced locally and nationally problems that were swept under the rug will slowly be brought to light.

While shepherds collectively (in the direct-democracy) compose the domestic national government, it would not be wise to give them the power to appoint members of the Federal Reserve because the shepherds carry the potential to keep interest rates abnormally high to increase their own funding. Therefore, when we consider a new international body to have the job of maintaining the role of the Federal Reserve, we need to consider which people have the greatest interest in and understanding of how the stocks and bonds market performs.

In general, the two greatest stakeholders are the banking industry on the one hand, and the hundreds of thousands of individual stockholders, on the other, who owe their financial well-being, whether it be through employment or their retirement funds, to the stability and growth of the market. In any election, there are candidates, and there are voters. These two parties supply the candidates from the leading banks among the member nations as well as hundreds of thousands of stockholders votes. Each stockholder represents partial ownership of an industry, and each industry represents part of the business economy. Each stock market represents a certain percentage of the world economy, and collectively the markets, businesses, and industries represent the economy itself in such a way that each stockholder in some way owns not only a piece of an industry but also part of the whole economy. The more shares they own, the greater investment they have in the economy, and therefore, the greater voice they have among the various candidates selected.

...for the Capitalist

However, if we allowed banks to be the only source of candidates, we would fail to recognize that the financial market has evolved into many other kinds of financial institutions. Some of them include accounting firms, stock trading corporations, mutual fund corporations, credit card companies, and credit bureaus. Therefore, it seems only prudent that the best of these industries also be allowed to submit candidates for a vote among the stockholders. After the market has selected their thirteen members, then they may select one member as *Wizard* of the board.

At the time of the creation of the Federal Reserve, many saw its power as the threat to the power of the people. One such book on this was *the Wizard of Oz*. As many ideas have been fashioned from those original criticisms, it seems only proper to name our new reserve the Oz Reserve.[11] As we analyze human history, we take note that all too often the strong prey upon the weak. In the beginning, it started out with physical strength, and today, strength comes from one's monetary value in terms of assets and bank accounts as well as political positions of power. Corporate democracy has several evils that we cannot ignore, for the votes of the wealthy, in terms of shareholders, are significantly greater than the votes of the poor. We have allowed this to preserve the capitalist system (the founding father's rights of the minority) as well as their hopes and dreams. Not to neglect their knowledge of the stock market and the economy is essential to the lives of trillions of people. There is an even greater risk that the right to own stock will become eventually more of an exclusive club or oligopoly. Therefore, the stock trading companies, mutual fund organizations and others by design have now been placed in competition to place candidates on the ballot for the Oz Reserve Board. To accomplish this, each candidate will be selected from among the organizations that are able to get the maximum amount of public voice in the market in terms of the customers they serve. Of course, this is one of many criteria we have put in place. Our underlying goal is to allow the public to determine the organizations of which the candidates will be selected simply by where and whom they choose to invest with. As the proxy votes, in this case, are public, if the people do not like how the board of directors' votes for specific candidates they can boycott those products and or services, unions also reserve the right to strike, and the people themselves still retain the power to create law should the Oz reserve overstep its bounds.

We also realize that the Oz Reserve itself, as is the case with any institution, must evolve and grow in a healthy manner. Governments individually have often resorted to printing currency when they get into a financial jam. We also have realized that our businesses are truly becoming international. While it is easy for larger businesses to use their capital to expand in foreign nations, smaller businesses find it very difficult to receive loans from the banking establishments in their *home* nation to expand to *foreign* nations abroad. Equally problematic, foreign nations hesitate to loan capital to foreigners as the possibility of such loans takes on the risk of having our foreigner take the money and return to his home nation where he is beyond the powers of foreign national law. Therefore, it is necessary that the Oz Reserve be designed as a multinational institution. The problem with this is that the Oz Reserve, like other

---

[11] Also see *the Oz Principle*, By Craig Hickman, 1994

PRIVATIZATION OF GOVERNMENT

institutions, requires laws and boundaries so that its powers do not expand upon their legal boundaries or the sovereignty of member nations. The problem with setting up boundaries and laws on multinational institutions is that it becomes difficult for us to enforce our democratic ideals of the Jezreel law-creation process on other sovereign nations that do not represent their people as well as our own form of government. To allow each nation, a voice in how the Oz Reserve conducts itself as well as maintain our democratic ideals in the same method that was used to elect our members of the Oz Reserve Board will also be used to pass laws governing the board. When considering the prospect of a global currency, many have entertained the prospect of an international congress or a head of state with law making options. The problem with these options is that they significantly take the public voice outside of the equation. By retaining a stockholder's vote, from stockholders of all the member nations, for any changes made to the Oz Reserve, we are still keeping the process democratic through the vote, rather than an appointed position. It is also important to note that those involved most heavily in the vote have the greatest knowledge and background in the economic and financial needs of the day. In addition, to enforce the integrity of the individual sovereign nations, we can allow each nation to propose a limited number of market and banking proposals to the stockholders' vote. This also allows Jezreel to follow its democratic ideals behind the laws that the democracy proposes. Therefore, the method chosen will be the same as a Kingdom Decree proposal, whereby the proposal with the greatest number of signatures may be presented for a stockholders vote. Other modifications have been made as well to ensure the public's voice in the process. Some of the members of the Oz Reserve Board were selected from the stock trading companies that have the most transactions and with the greatest number of clients. This was done in an effort to encourage those who trade stock to bring the public as much as possible into the process.

For those of you who do not know, the Federal Reserve sets the interest rate by which money may be borrowed from the government itself. The new government creates savings for each city locally—those funds as part of the surplus that is not used by the lord nor by the shepherd. This provides the government an avenue by which it can receive interest on its own saving while also providing loans to the population. Of course, each nation will be required to provide funds in their own manner, however, republics that continually run into occasional debts, or even annual deficits, as is the case in the United States, are left in such a position that they need to borrow money to allow their banking industry people to borrow funds. Unfortunately, often what countries do is print more currency, which in turn lowers the value of the currency in use. But to prevent this from taking place, each of the mints is to be disbursed among the participating nations in the Oz Reserve so that each of the mints is held accountable by the other member nation-states.

Given the threat of inflation, under what circumstances is it important to print money and what safeguards can we put in place during such times? If one looks at the continual deficits within the United States, the question comes to mind who are they borrowing the money from? The answer is the US Central Bank, but the Central Bank does not have the kind of trillions of dollars the government routinely demands so they just print the money thus a slow annal inflationary gain is created, but because the US Central Bank charges interest on the money given the US Government is hesitant to print too much money.

During times of great economic disaster government borrows significantly more, thus the printing of money grows proportionately higher. Two examples come to mind in terms of causes of economic disasters, these two are wars and medical epidemics. When people are scared, they stop spending and/or they are prevented from spending due to the crisis. For instance, during a quarantine movement is restricted and during war people are scared to leave their homes. During a depression industries and businesses go into bankruptcy and tax revenue plummets. And yet during such times money is needed the most to increase employment. For instance, during a war money is needed for defense, and during a medical epidemic funds are needed for hospitals. During such times, the national and local governments will also need to be infused with capital to ensure that even if people cannot pay their bills, the lights stay on, and public order is maintained through law enforcement. These options are put in place by degrees in proportion to the severity of the circumstances. The private sector is more productive than the public sector in a good economy, but as the economy collapses the need for production moves to the public sector. Thus, when a state of emergency is declared by the member nations of the Oz Reserve the power of the money supply will shift in proportion to the vote to the public sector. Shepherds and lords have an abundance of projects that they would like to do but are limited by the revenue received. By infusing them with capital, without the threat of interest, all these projects may be unleashed simultaneously to give the economy the boost it requires. As stability returns, the market funds re-enter the banking system and things return to normal. Thus, unlike the United States, which prints money in good years and the bad through their annual deficits, the government is prevented from receiving such payouts without a state of emergency thus allowing the private sector to grow unhindered, while still allowing the safeguards in place in case of a dramatic economic upheaval.

Now there has been some discussion of a cashless society. There are several advantages and disadvantages to consider. Most evil in the world comes down to a desire for wealth. People will steal, fraud, extort, and murder for it. Cash is used for most illegal ventures because it is difficult to track, without cash; every transaction would be noted, allowing law enforcement to follow the electronic money to the source. Cash, however, is, for the most part, an anonymous transfer of wealth, which makes it desirable for the criminal element in society. Credit card transactions could be made much more secure by authenticating a thumbprint for each transaction as opposed to a signature. Checks & Credit Cards, in like manner, could also contain a person's photo, use a bar-code for the routing, and account information for instant-cashing. Using our proposed DNA Identification for citizens, there exists a possibility to use DNA ID for all business transactions as well. Your DNA is unique to identify you and you alone. You would not need to carry a wallet because you carry it with you wherever you go. While these are positive attributes for businesses, to reduce crime, and I am seriously considering many of them in our new society, there are some very big negative losses to individual liberty by removing cash from society. You cannot directly transfer a credit card between people efficiently. You can give someone a check, but then you are forcing him or her with the inconvenience of having to go to the bank to cash or deposit the check. Until these inconveniences are overcome, we are stuck with the present currency system for better or worse. I bring these thoughts up to elicit your thoughts on possible alternative options to this dilemma.

Yet this brings us to another dilemma. A stockholder is an owner of at least part of an organization. If the Oz Reserve could set standards for loans or bankruptcy laws, it is expected that the plight of the poor would be ignored or significantly hampered as the nature of the business world is to expand profits often with a blind eye to the effects or cost to society. A popular corporate phrase many have probably heard is, *it's just business* when attempting to justify one's moral conscience to the hurt one business causes another entity, be it a person, community, business or society. Jefferson once said, "*I believe that banking institutions are more dangerous to our liberties than standing armies. Already they have risen up a moneyed aristocracy that has set the Government at defiance. The issuing power should be taken from the banks and restored to the people to whom it properly belongs.*"[12]

The direct-democracy system itself, by starting the law-creation process at the bottom and using that plan as a model and reference point, must combat the divisions in humanity that empower the few over the many. However, we must account for several difficulties when dealing with our new multinational banking and other financial institutions. If bankruptcy laws and laws governing the loans, for example, were developed individually, nation-by-nation, but the impact of those laws was felt by all member nations conflicts and factions would inevitably develop that would gradually erode the bonds of friendship and unity. However, we also account for the fact that not all nations are democracies. The goal of true democracy is to shine like a lighthouse, in effect to draw nations and peoples to adopt this form of government through want and desire, rather than through force of legal obligation or war. This means that each member nation must be allowed to accept the multinational financial laws or reject them in their own way. Yet we still need to ensure our democratic ideals are maintained. Therefore, we have stipulated that our multinational banking laws will be written by a multinational body; we refer to as the *Commission of Uniform Banking Standards.* However, the laws must be accepted by the people, in the democracy, before they become the law of the land. How other member nations choose to accept or reject such laws is up to them. This allows this new form of government to retain the guiding light for the people while maintaining the sovereignty of member nations.

The City Lord and Budget

You may have noticed by now that we have put a major effort into planning to maximize the rights of the local governments across the spectrum, from the creation of law to the general finance of national and local budgets.[13] Anytime finances of the

---

[12] In Defense of Democracy, <etext.virginia.edu/jefferson/quotations/>, Letter to William Stevens Smith (November 13, 1787), quoted in Padover's *Jefferson on Democracy*, <en.wikiquote.org/wiki/Thomas_Jefferson>.
[13] History of Judah 39:16.

amounts used by governments are under consideration; one must be prudent about those tax dollars. Governments are different from businesses because when a business receives funds, that money belongs to that business, but when a government receives funds, that money really still belongs to the people. Unlike most businesses, the financial purpose of government is not just to increase revenues, but rather to use the funding collected for the welfare and well-being of the people. When taxes have come from families that may have needed those funds for food or medicine, every dollar becomes crucial. For these reasons, it is essential that we use efficiently all government funds today, and adequately save, to prepare for the needs of our kin and their kin, and so on, so that those who come after us will always have enough for what they need, and there will be a free and prosperous country unburdened by a huge national debt. In this matter also, we follow Thomas Jefferson's advice, for he said, *"Loading up the nation with debt and leaving it for the following generations to pay is morally irresponsible. Excessive debt is a means by which governments oppress the people and waste their substance. No nation has a right to contract a debt for periods longer than the majority contracting it can expect to live ... I sincerely believe ... that the principle of spending money to be paid by posterity under the name of funding is but swindling futurity on a large-scale."* [14]

    Let's say a lord has a forty percent surplus and the national government can take fifty percent of that surplus; twenty percent of the city's budget remains for long-term savings, which then can be made available for anything from national disasters to war—God forbid—when the kingdom could find itself in a real economic crisis. The result is that we shift from a political system that functions on deficits (as in the United States) to one that functions on surplus savings. Of course, the amount of the savings will vary greatly from one city to the next, but when averaged together these savings, long-term, will be for, the whole country, a great advantage. This consideration helps to explain why the city budget is always so important: It provides the funding for all the direct-democracy's internal needs.

    Independent Class citizenship has been, at least in part, tied to employment. This caveat is only of value if there exists real employment opportunities within the nation. However, in cases of true economic depression, no work exists for the ready, willing, and able. Under such circumstances, such rules have no logical place, and therefore under such conditions, the class restrictions to voting have been waived. Yet there are still other considerations. For example, the city allows taxation through property tax and\or income taxes. The problem with this is that often a person will live in one city and work in another. So where should a person be able to vote for a lordship candidate where he or she lives and pays property taxes or where he or she works and pays income taxes? The problem is that if we do either one, but not both we are punishing one, or at least, denying them a voice in the taxes they pay. For this reason, people who work in the city will be allowed to vote for their income tax percentage, and people who live in the city will be allowed to vote for their property tax percentage. Of course, we do not want people voting twice for the same candidates

---

[14] In Defense of Democracy, <etext.virginia.edu/jefferson/quotations/>, Letter to William Stevens Smith (November 13, 1787), quoted in Padover's *Jefferson on Democracy*, <en.wikiquote.org/wiki/Thomas_Jefferson>.

either, but using modern technology, biometrics, etc., these risks can be minimized or altogether eliminated.

For the moment and for the sake of argument, let us remove economic fluctuations, natural disasters, and other such major variables things from the economic equation and see, for the moment, the economy as in a steady state. When a lord puts his budget and tax rate on the ballot, he thereby becomes politically responsible for the safety and well-being of his own people, within his town, because it is his budget that provides for the police, fire, road maintenance, and other such public services. If his budget gets to the point where the various public services can no longer be provided due to negligent or inappropriate fund usage, the system in that city, at least, has failed its people, and there is nothing more elemental to a system of government than the safety and well-being of its people. By holding a lord financially accountable to his city for his own budgetary incompetence, the lord has a major incentive to perform well and to do what is right. By removing the city council and putting the budget directly under the authority of a single lord, all the weight of success or failure falls upon one person. As it is written, "Many shepherds will ruin my vineyard[15], "which is also in line with Jefferson's advice, where he said: *Responsibility weighs with its heaviest force on a single head ... I think history furnishes as many examples of a single usurper arising out of a government by a plurality as of temporary trust of power in a single hand rendered permanent by usurpation. I do not believe, therefore, that this danger is lessened in the hands of a plural Executive (city council). Perhaps it is greatly increased by the state of inefficiency to which they are liable from feuds and divisions among themselves.*[16]

Unfortunately, if police or other public safety services are not present, or if there is not good management of some major city service, disruptive disaster and especially its aftermath, looting and rioting may occur, or there may be widespread panic, and people will be needlessly hurt or killed, and holding the lord accountable for mismanagement of these emergency services will not repair the damage. For these reasons, the national government must be able to step in when there are dire conditions for which the lords' powers are not sufficient to meet the needs. I have discussed the benefits of introducing competition into the lord's budget, yet let's say the elected lord spends all his budget, including his surplus. Without funds all city functions stop. Under such circumstances we can expect such riots and looting. Thus, we must have a process that allows the lords to fail, as to weed out the incompetent ones, but never allows the cities to fail so that order is always maintained, and essential public services continue in a solvent manner. To meet these ends among the realms is our Oz realm who will take financial control over the city if it is unable to provide for its most essential necessities, childhood education, police, fire, etc. Its priority is to perform an investigation into the city's financial records. What was the cause of the financial failure. Was the lord or a member of his staff siphoning the cities resources for personal benefit? Perhaps the lord was not to blame and was undermined in some way. Perhaps the city's or shire's jurisdiction is too small to

---

[15] Jeremiah 12:10.
[16] In Defense of Democracy, <etext.virginia.edu/jefferson/quotations/>, Letter to William Stevens Smith (November 13, 1787), quoted in Padover's *Jefferson on Democracy*, <en.wikiquote.org/wiki/Thomas_Jefferson>.

support its population and needs to be reorganized. Oz is to have a local townhall meeting to hear from the public. A solution is to be brought forward for the long-term viability of the city. Oz like most realms has its own set of courts should charges need to be brought against any entity for malfeasance. In this way the viability of the city is maintained, while corruption is systematically weeded out.

The use of forced taxation in the current republic system of government allows gross waste in city and state funding to be masked as politicians may get taxes increased if they so desire when they get into a financial jam, rather than careful scrutiny and in-depth research of the present spending. For many years in Los Angeles supervisors received their pay by how many people were employed under them. This created a situation where supervisors had an incentive to hire more personnel, whether the need existed or not. By creating a system of public choice in advance over taxation, we attempt to bring the element of competition, as used in the private sector, to improve the efficiency of city governments. However, when we say, "bring the element of competition," we do not mean putting business in charge of government, but rather we mean using capitalistic business principles to promote competition among different budget proposals through the candidates for lord, a plan which should maximize the value of each dollar spent through government funding.

There is a fundamental fact about government spending that most people do not fully understand. If we look at the spending levels of the city government of just one city, it will seem small when compared with the state (or realm) government spending, and if we look at state (or realm) government spending, that in turn will seem small when compared with national government spending. Therefore, in the present system when the media spotlight wasteful spending, almost invariably they concentrate on the spending done by the national government, such as "the bridge to nowhere" in Alaska ridiculed by Senator John McCain. In a republic form of government, we take this approach naturally because the power base is at the top rather than the bottom, and because a small alteration in national funding could mean a difference of millions—or even billions—of tax dollars. Still, when we do this, we are closing our eyes to the greater issue.

To understand this more simply, let's think about the previous example. However, instead of comparing the national budget to one state (or realm) budget, let's compare the national government to the collective budgets of all fifty states. When we do this, the figures are reversed, and, amazingly, it is now the national government's budget that looks small in comparison! It is the same also when we compare the collective city budgets from across the nation with the collective state (or realm) budgets. The more one understands the vast amount of funds that are used by all the local government collectively; the more important the local city budgets appear to us. Naturally, the public is concerned about fraudulent spending, but it tends to focus almost exclusively (and wrongly) on the wastes and abuses of power and funding in the national government rather than ever noticing what is happening with wasted funds and abuses of power locally and regionally, at the city and state levels. Those vitally important problems tend to drift by unnoticed. However, by allowing the public to choose its own tax rate, and by increasing the real power of the local population, the focus of government funding will be shifted from far-away national events to the hometown scene. In this way, we hope to make inefficiency and corruption in the whole political system much more transparently obvious to the public.

One of the primary complaints against a direct-democracy system is that the Congress, the state legislature, and even the city council pass a great many bills that often go unnoticed as trivial, but do have a beneficial impact on society. When we analyze the content of these bills passed through these legislative bodies, we find that most of them fall into two general categories, codes, and standards, which we will discuss in section four, and the area of budget priorities and funding, be it in the city, state, or national level. Unfortunately for the republic, many of these laws may be counterproductive, because often they establish government funding for programs that continue in use long after their useful life or suffer from redundancy of similar government programs as one member of Congress is not always aware of what his fellow congressmen are doing, where the left-hand does not see the right hand or vice-versa. In this new system, removing the bulk of these laws allows the lord, as one person, the flexibility to maneuver funds quickly, as a manager in the business world would do, to attend quickly to the needs of the city. The same is true for the shepherds. Now as the public views the actions of the lord or the Shepherd regarding their budgets, the people, through the laws they enact, will put the restraints they see as justified on the lords' budgets. Now it is also important to remember that because the lordship candidates are in competition with each other to lower taxation at the time of the public vote, they will have no valid methods for seeking subsequently new funds because unlike the senators and representatives in Congress, they only hurt themselves by approving wasteful spending.

Once again, however, our proposed solution seems to have a fundamental issue. Since the campaign for office is typically a five to six-month strenuous endeavor, the acting lord is controlling the city budget while he or she is also a candidate with a new city budget. Further complicating the matter, the lord's term of office in most governments does not end until about two months after the election. These delays are normal, so that all the votes may be counted accurately, any election disputes settled, and the whole election process officially certified. What, then, may stop the lord from blowing the surplus during these last months before the election, or, even more importantly, right after the election, in the remaining *lame duck* session?

Each lordship position is designed to be a coveted political office, but if the lord runs for re-election and wins by violating his or her budget, this malfeasance undermines the monetary foundations of democracy itself. Elections build up people's passion. Immediately following an election is roughly the most difficult time to oust any political figure, including a lord. The Oz Shepherd also may get votes from a lord's city, which makes it difficult politically for the Oz Shepherd to remove a lord from office right after an election. Then there is political party favoritism, where the Oz Shepherd may be inclined to look in the other direction should the violating lord be a popular member of his own political party. In theory, the Oz Shepherd has a financial incentive to prosecute the sitting lord, but the people have just elected the lord, and at that time normally everyone is eager to set politics aside for a while. Also, there may be a new Oz Shepherd who is taking his or her seat and may be reluctant to act. Political transition periods are always difficult times, with so many diverse things going on around the kingdom, and each election can radically alter the direction of the shire or Kingdom, depending on who is in office. To make the situation more difficult, these transitions do not take place one at a time, but rather all at once. However, just saying that a lord needs to keep his or her budget in line is not enough. Laws without enforcement become meaningless, and for all practical purposes, they might as well not exist. In this case, when we think about enforcement what we most need to look at is who has an incentive to enforce the law about lords and their budgets? To answer this question, we need to think about how the political party system works.

In most cities, people tend to be conservative or liberal, and typically most people belong to one party or another. We also know that, unfortunately, many of these voters tend to vote along party lines, rather than more carefully considering each candidate. This is the same basic issue about voting that republics have always had: *Voters tend to go for candidates rather than the candidates' proposals, plans, and priorities.* Be that as it may, we must accept the fact that the political two-party system is the dominant political reality in most developed countries of the world, and whether we agree or disagree, and whether we like it, probably it will stay around for a long time to come. Later, as we move along here, we will be researching several possible ways to disestablish the two-party system in favor of a three- or four-party system common in many nations in Europe as well as presently emerging in Mexico. After the Egyptian revolution, numerous Egyptian candidates ran to attempt to improve their country. The two with the most votes had a runoff election. However, most voters voted for neither of the two candidates that made it to the runoff election. To ensure all the people get the type of candidates they desire the most, this new system allows the voter to rank the candidates by order of preference so that those who voted for the candidate with the least number of votes, their vote will be applied to their second-place candidate. If both their first and second-place candidate received insufficient votes their vote will go to their third-place candidate, and so on, etc., until the greatest consensus possible is placed on the candidate that wins the election.

The Underdog

In the original US Constitution, there were no vice-presidential candidates, only presidential candidates. The candidate with the most votes became the president and second place became the vice president. Thus, the vice-president was intended to be a check on the powers of the president. The idea was that the vice president represented the minority and the founding fathers wanted to preserve the rights of the minority from the power of the majority. In this case the office of the president representing the will of the majority. Thus, the role of the Senate was to ensure that not only the rights of the states were preserved, but also the rights of the minority citizens that did not vote for the sitting president. To accomplish this, they gave the vice president a distinguished role in the Senate to preserve the rights of the minority. My intention is to re-establish this check on leadership in both the local, national, and

PRIVATIZATION OF GOVERNMENT

international levels of government. On the local level to keep the lord in check, on the national level to keep the shepherd in check, and on the international level to keep the prince in check. Such positions only have merit if they have an avenue, such as through the Senate in a Republic, to preserve the rights of the minority. My priority then is to analyze the structure and need within the government to maximum effect.

The city enforces the law through the Police Department, City Inspectors, and an apparatus of other city officials. Laws are put in place to prevent those administrating the law from abusing that privilege, however, when that privilege is abused the John and Jane Doe citizen have very little authority over the heavy hand of the city's law enforcement agencies. Without the presence of a city council how do we prevent the lord from abusing his office? Whether a country has a two-party system or a ten-party system, the political party process itself tends to spark bitter rivalries between and among the candidates. Each candidate may instinctively do everything possible to make the other candidate fail, such as with personal attacks, although, I like to believe, most voters are much more interested in the issues than the political soap opera. Also, where open primaries are allowed, people will sometimes vote for candidates they dislike but believe they will be able to defeat their opposing candidate in the general election. My solution to the previous matter we discussed would be to allow the Underdog (first runner-up aka 2nd place candidate for lord) to take the place of the lord in case the lord violates his or her budget surplus allotment within the six months prior to the election, or immediately thereafter, following the election near the end of the term. The Underdog could accomplish this through the Oz Court system. The Oz Court system is used over the shire court system as the Oz Judge would be able to make a sound decision without fear of local impeachment looming over the trial that may impair any verdict the judge may render. Also, as the Oz Judge receives his funding from the national government, the judge will likely take lordship violators to such funding more seriously. Lords who violate their budget are not allowed to run for public office again. This gives the runner-up lord; the one who lost in the election, a tremendous incentive to make sure that the elected lord is abiding by all the rules. Just the threat of getting replaced by a candidate from the opposite political party would give the elected lord an incentive to either get that budget in line or to not run, to not be ousted by the opposition. Then, should the Underdog assume the office, nothing will be easy because many will see this route into office as somehow tainted or not quite legitimate, and it may be the first-time in a long while that a candidate from that party has been a lord of that city. In sum, these rules provide significant incentives but also leave the candidates with much to prove.

Spending is easier than savings, and it is easier to destroy than to build; a bad lord, with a faulty budget, government waste, neglect, mismanagement can quickly destroy a local economy in months that took decades to establish. Therefore, the initial term for new lords is shorter to get those with poor budgeting skills out of the system fast, while we reward those with budgetary prudence longer terms in office.

These circumstances may also put the sitting lord into a desperate situation, and in that case, he or she will use every legal option to increase the city's funds. While there are several benefits to the initial flexibility for government spending, we must also realize that if the lord were to find alternative methods of taxation combined with flexible spending, the consequences could be disastrous. For example, cities are usually responsible for providing electricity, water, sewer, and trash disposal to the residents. If the lord could increase these charges at will, then, by using other methods to gather revenue, this would bypass the previously submitted tax rate on the ballot. This is not an unrealistic threat because the present system of government in most nations has many different ways to tax. This list includes, but is not limited to: hotel tax, rental car tax, sales tax, income tax, property tax, electrical tax, water tax, corporate tax, telephone tax, luxury tax, cigarette tax, social security tax, Medicare tax, permit fees, toll roads and bridges, parking meters, and inspection fees. Sadly, today, many towns and cities have turned to covert actions such as using traffic citations as a source of extra revenue. Some towns even have a tax on food. Is there anything we do that is not—in some way, shape, or form—taxed? In our new system of government, all services provided by the city must be funded by the income and or property tax percentage that the lord formally proposes on the ballot. What we attempt to do, then, is to reduce the city's manifest control over its population by making it beneficial for the lord to privatize city functions and thereby cut spending. Why should city taxes be increased because a lord has planned poorly? In this way, at least the service will continue to function, and it will go on when the budgetary funds are no longer sufficient.

Remember, also, since the people themselves make the laws, they may choose through the vote which services the lord may privatize and which ones must remain public. Still, we need to realize that some city functions such as police, fire, and emergency health services may become corrupted (such as by greed) or inefficient when they are delegated as a monopoly to the private sector. Because of this consideration, we have left the several city functions that must remain public, except, once again, possibly, through a public vote. It is easy to want to mandate some of these functions to the private or public-sector, but if we do so, we may well be moving in opposition to our direct-democracy goals to empower the will of the people. Remember as well that direct-democracy does not mean that the people will make the right decisions; it means that the people alone will be responsible for their own decisions.

Providing capitalist consequences for overspending is not enough, the reverse need is there, and there must be some significant reward for provident, sufficient saving. By allowing only incumbent lords to retain the savings they have earned from their previous term(s) in office, we apportion to them a huge electoral advantage. In this way, they can promise infrastructure for tomorrow's technologies and other improvements to the city that other candidates cannot. If a lordship incumbent can run continually with a surplus, even a slight one, that lord has manifested fiscal responsibility with the people's funds. Therefore, such lords should have a good chance to extend their terms of office should they decide to run again. For us, this does several things. First, for larger city projects, such as the building and construction of museums, observatories, zoos, stadiums, and other public facilities, it will take time to save and set aside the necessary funds. Remember, we are moving away from a system of borrowing and towards a system of saving. Also, the more often a lord wins' reelection, the greater his or her name recognition will be, and the more his popularity will grow so that with each passing year it becomes increasingly difficult at election time for a challenger to oust the incumbent from office.

So then, by making the terms in office shorter at the beginning, we hope that the process will weed out any lords who rush to judgment and tend to make poor strategic decisions. Alternatively, on the other hand, a veteran lord with many good years of experience will be able to save and invest in larger, long-term city projects for the good of all the people.[17]

This may at first sound strange, but the budget and how the money is spent could be much more important than the candidates themselves. Because the candidates are elected to office, we know that to at least some degree the people of that town have chosen the person for elected office. Now we must believe that a candidate is only as good as the candidate's word. When lords are unable to maintain the city budget—even with a forty percent surplus in anticipation of unexpected budgetary fluctuations—they are in violation of their word to the people of the city. Perhaps the consequences for major budgetary violations seem harsh, but those who have been elected to public office have been entrusted with much, and, as the adage goes, "To whom much is given, much is expected." Since the lords and the shepherds represent the nation's economic infrastructure, keeping their decisions in line with their budgets is a significant fundamental financial need of any government.

Theoretically, what we anticipate is having a radical internal change during the early new lordship terms because the tax rates may be too low to provide for the needs of the city government.[18] As we mentioned previously, the shire governments will be moving tentatively to see what works, and there will be some trial-and-error in how the municipal governments are managed. The people, attempting to embrace their new power in the system, will add energy to this dynamic, producing even more volatility. When the next election cycle comes along, cities that were left totally underfunded will go in the reverse direction, with a new lord and much higher taxes, resulting in a tax hike too large for the city's needs. However, there will have also been some successful lords able to maintain a good, stable order. In fact, just hearing about the various disorders in other cities will keep many lords on edge and more careful about how each tax dollar is spent. As understanding evolves and there is a better sense of the new responsibilities that the job of lord now entails, and after those in office see the consequences to unsuccessful lords from the government of the realms, the public's views will change about what kind of candidates for lord they want. In the republic using forced taxation, incoming mayors (lords) can essentially leave the system on autopilot and know that they will have enough funds to meet their needs. However, this method—while it does provide some stability—also encourages waste. Over the years this tradition of supposedly "benign neglect" slowly builds like sludge and becomes worse, hampering operations. Also, when the public wants further or better services, they present propositions known as bond measures with essentially the buy-now-and-pay-later approach. In this new system

---

[17] Matthew 25:19-21.

[18] Why would voluntary methods fail to work under our present system? <capitalism.org/faq/taxation.htm>.

of government, the people may require by the vote whatever facilities they want from the shire government, but it will be the responsibility of each lord to provide for those projects or services through their budget with buy-now, pay-now. Remember, this new position for lords, who are central to the whole structure of the direct-democracy system of government, was never intended to be easy. Due to the rigid requirements and standards that the position entitles, we can also expect that the amount of research and study that will go into any run for office will significantly increase to the point where college classes and books about managing cities will become commonplace. As the quality of the candidates improves, the safety and security of the community will improve as well. Over the long-term, saving from the lords will increase, and with that should come civil and infrastructure improvements that will enhance community long-term growth and well-being. The government of the realms, because they rely on the city governments for funding, will also become adept at analyzing the cities' budgets, thus allowing them to identify problem areas sooner, rather than later, and over the course of time the government of the realm will be able to verify that the fundamental reasons for using a surplus are being maintained. This is sure to happen because a violation to these required surpluses will cause the realms to lose their own revenue.

Shire Judges

For each one of these checks and balances to function most effectively, the design must be such that each constituent group has some internal need or desire to enforce the law as well as it is possible in practical terms to do so. U.S. founding father James Madison referred to this arrangement as *using ambition to counteract ambition*. It is not enough to make a government about of things we desire, but instead, we must also create an environment wherein the natural instincts of humankind will naturally encourage the social results we want to see. For example, we know that all societies need judges, but if a city lord could appoint judges, then the judges might have the wrong political incentives to look the other way if the lord breaks the law or to support the lord and ergo the city government over the needs of the people. This follows the age-old principle of "not biting the hand that feeds you." Alternatively, judges could run for public office, and the people, with their vote, could decide, which is the current method. Nevertheless, that is not a good method because most voters do not know or research the judges on the ballot, and so their votes are not intelligent and responsible.

The solution we propose is to allow the runner-up lordship candidate, the Underdog, to appoint the city judges, with those appointments also being subject to confirmation by a majority of lords in the Shire Fellowship. This plan should work well for several reasons. First, by having the judges appointed by the lord's chief competitor, they are more apt to prosecute the lord and \ or city officials for any wrongdoing. We also know that these candidates for the bench have stood up to the scrutiny of the lords on the Shire Fellowship.

Of course, the judges must remain accountable to the people of the city or shire where they serve. Judicial service in a republic is a lifetime position. How, then, can we confirm that a judge will always remain accountable to the people? If we elect our judges, as is done in a republic, will that translate into good representation with effective enforcement of the laws? The challenge is that when they vote for or against them, most people do not know who the judges are. To understand this better, it is important to understand also the basic concepts of the judicial system. As the old saying goes, "Justice is blind;" for a judge to render an opinion on a case without knowing all the facts is exactly contrary to the profession's own standards. This also makes it difficult to know where judges stand on the issues, and this also makes a direct vote impractical. Unlike most political statements of candidates, judges' decisions are often finely nuanced, and when candidates run for office, they are usually running on the issues—the very thing that judges find difficult to discuss in a political context. Therefore, judges make the worst candidates on the ballot because few people know where, exactly, they stand on most of the issues. When a judge is on the ballot for a recall vote, then, at least, the public has something to compare the judge against. Typically, judges are recalled due to some unfavorable decision where some form of judicial prejudice or bias is felt which tainted the verdict(s). Often such drastic measures are not the result of a single inappropriate verdict, but rather through a pattern of preserve abuse from the bench. Our goal is to have judges that rule with the most equitable justice, according to law, who also enforce the will of the people rather than special interests, power, or privilege. In this way, then, the people will come to know, trust, and understand their judges.

Thus, whereas the people do not elect judges to the bench, they have the power to remove them. For this reason, also, judges will have a strong incentive to serve well, as indicated above. Now the Underdog may not select just anyone to be a judge. Appointments may be determined through Shire Law (i.e., public vote), but some minimum qualification should be a law degree from an accredited university or from those who have sponsored propositions that became law in that shire. For those who have sponsored shire laws, this helps to ensure that those laws will be enforced. While the people did not vote for these people, the people did vote for their propositions to become law. This will allow us to have confidence that these judges, being original successful sponsors, will have the support of the people, should those judges ever have to rule on the fate of a lord or other high-ranking city official(s). Sponsors of proposals that have become law have clearly defined positions on issues, and especially their main issue after a confirming vote from the people makes their proposition law. In this manner, the public has indirectly approved them as a judge through the passage of their ideas on the ballot. It is equally important that candidates have broad levels of knowledge and background in the judicial system. Therefore, there are two kinds of judicial candidates for this selection, namely, one for the enforcement of new laws and one for the enforcement and understanding of historical laws.

By granting the Underdogs the power to appoint judges, this further empowers the multiple party system, which proceeds more by proportion rather than winner-take-all. Statistics about elections show a strong bias in favor of incumbents, and, besides that, they show that the longer politicians remain in office, the more difficult they become to uproot. People are creatures of habit, and they tend to become uncritical about, and comfortable, with the way things are, which may be disadvantageous. Our design provides also that the better the job the lord performs in economic terms, the longer his or her term in office may be. The ability to appoint judges is a huge win, then, for those who do not quite succeed in making it into the lordship position. Also, this design creates a strong incentive for candidates to run who know that they have little real chance of winning the lordship position. This plan also creates a foundational opening for other parties to enter the arena, for they only need to get enough votes for second-place to have the power to put their appointments into judicial positions. By putting in place a set of checks and balances on the judge, the Shire Fellowship (made up of the lords) has an inherent rationale not to trust these judges, even though they are responsible for confirming them. This process also allows the Shire Fellowship to analyze and screen carefully the accreditations and qualifications of all judges before they take the bench, right from the beginning of the selection process.

While we believe the city courts to be sufficient staying true to our democratic ideals, we allow any shire to create private courts as determined by public vote.

From the previous section, we recalled that the original designers of the U.S. Constitution thought in terms of states much smaller than we have today in the U.S.A. The primary difference between a state and a shire must be that a shire, being smaller, allows the people living there to have a better overall understanding of the needs, interests, and general outlook of most people who live there. The state, on the other hand, amounts to a landmass large enough to encompass the commercial infrastructure and cultural needs of the internal shires. For instance, the people of Los Angeles County (Shire) naturally have a greater understanding of the needs of the general Los Angeles area than they do those of Riverside County (Shire), and vice-versa. Therefore, to maximize the quality of their representation, they should be two separate shires. At the same time, these two shires are linked together by extensive freeways and roads, railways and commercial links, agreements, and bonds. They also utilize the same nuclear generators and wind turbines, aqueducts, and other economic infrastructure features, as well as shared universities, and medical facilities. As the state takes on the needs of institutions, infrastructure, and commerce ventures that are not efficiently accomplished or cost-effective when done by the shire government or the private sector, it becomes the infrastructural "glue" that effectively can bind the shires together. When Americans think of states, they may be thinking about places on the eastern seaboard such as Delaware or Rhode Island, but what we have in mind here are much larger political units. However, in Kingdom, our terms change, ergo, instead of *states,* we dub them *realms*. Therefore, according to the definitions and usage of this book, we will consider *large states*—in terms of both landmass and total population—such as California, Texas, Pennsylvania, and New York to be *realms*, whereas we will be thinking of *smaller states*—again, in terms of both landmass and population—such as Wyoming, Rhode Island, and Delaware to be, by comparison, more like shires.

At this point, we have laid out the foundations for shire government in the direct-democracy model, but if the system is to function well, we need to explain also a few fundamental principles about shires and realms as such. First, to begin, to maintain a Shire Fellowship, there must be enough lords among whom to share overall authority

PRIVATIZATION OF GOVERNMENT

in the shire. Also, we need to determine how many people are needed at the city level to provide the services required to maintain courts, a police system, educational needs, and so forth. As it turns out, these questions are among the most difficult to answer. For this purpose, we establish several guidelines, but whether these numbers are too many or too few, only time will tell. Naturally, the outer extremes are of most concern. There could be cities with millions of people that should be further subdivided to represent everyone better, or tiny groups of say, ten to fifteen people attempting to denominate their group a city. These rules also need to have some flexibility, such that as populations grow, cities and shires may politically subdivide themselves better to maintain reasonable levels of representation. If we study the history of the U.S.A., we notice that the main issue about this was not that new states were originally too large. In fact, other than the original thirteen colonies, most states began as territories occupied chiefly by Indians, with few settlers from the original thirteen states. The issue was, and is, that after the westward expansion began, as the population increased, the size of the states tended to remain about the same. Oregon, California, and Texas, to name only three, would have been far more representative units for their populations if the states would have been allowed to divide further according to their actual representative needs. Texas, for instance, when annexed by the United States had a population of roughly 40,000. However, due to the westward expansion from the eastern states, Congress realized that the population of Texas would grow rapidly. Therefore the state was allowed and expected to divide itself into as many as five independent sovereign states to better represent the political divides of the day and age, which during those days was the issue of slavery.[19] Today the efforts made against state subdivision have nothing to do with representation but rather with national identity. In other words, people feel that those interested in subdividing a state are somehow not patriotic. However, with the new democratic model, if representation is to be improved, surely it is logical that shires should be able to subdivide. That is not to say that all shires should be small in landmass. The states of Alaska and Wyoming are excellent examples because they have large landmass but so little population that at some point subdivision would not allow the basic economic infrastructure of the shire government to be, in practical terms, self-sufficient.

This naturally brings on another fundamental issue. Shires are to be supported through city taxation, which also directly supports the needs of the cities. However, in terms of geography, not everyone lives within city limits. Similarly, there are people everywhere that live and sometimes regularly work beyond the boundaries of city limits; that said, there are rural populations, and these people still have the right to have their children receive an education in public-schools and the protection of timely law enforcement, fire protection, road maintenance, and other services. In the United States, for instance, the issue presents itself in many ways. These rural people include farmers, ranchers, miners, hip-hop hermits, etc., but they also may include many non-rural people who happen to live just outside city limits. My uncle lived in a

---

[19] Transcript of Compromise of 1850 -
<ourdocuments.gov/doc.php?flash=true&doc=27&page=transcript>

regular community in Washington state where his was the last house in a row. When the house was built, the city determined that his house happened to be just beyond the city limits, and because of this, the paved streets end just before his home. Also, while everyone else got their mail delivered to their homes, his went to a postal box, where routinely he had to pick it up at the downtown Post Office. Cities grow with their populations. Therefore, it seems logical and natural that the legal boundaries of the city should expand when the city expands, everything else being equal, such as water districts and water rights. As we have designed matters, the people who live on the outskirts of the city have a choice: Either they may be incorporated into an entirely new town, or they may be incorporated into the already existing, expanding city. Cities and realms are and must be dynamic entities relative to their populations. If a group of people in a specific geographic area believe that they are not well represented in their city or shire, and they, therefore, want to break off from that group and form their own new city or shire, then they should not have to go to the people who are being represented in the city or shire outside of the geographic area to ask for their permission to leave the city or shire. The only rules about this that are needed are that the group who want to form their own *town* should be sufficiently numerous, and they should all live adjacently, in the same geographical area, or at least within a very reasonable proximity. For people that would like to form their own *shire,* there should be no problem with that either, provided that all of those people live adjacently, in the same geographic area, or nearly so, and provided that there are at least a half-dozen cities that would be included in the whole new shire, and, at the same time, the former shire would still retain also at least a half-dozen cities. Thus, we envision a more fluid arrangement freely allowing for divisions and mergers between cities and shires, and such changes might be encouraged for the better representation, development, cooperation, and self-sufficiency of all the cities and shires. The creation of enclaves within towns and villages allows for practical boundaries where future divides between cities and towns may take place as the population increases. These natural boundaries give enclaves a natural unique identity and feeling of belonging so that when the population increases to a necessary level separation as their own representative town or city would become natural evolution.

The Shire Fellowship

We also need to consider that lords, and other local political entities rarely see eye to eye. There will always be lords that do not get along with each other, and shire governments may not get along with other shire governments. When these lords are in the same shire, the city courts or Shire Fellowship— depending on the circumstances—may intervene to make peace and find solutions. When they do not, the National Courts are available. Sometimes we know that certain situations require immediate attention. According to the nature of the dispute the corresponding shepherd is granted some authority to act as an intermediary between lords or shires involved, to be a peacemaker and arbitrate good solutions. As there are multiple realms, each with a different jurisdiction, the shepherd sent should correspond to the crisis at hand. For instance, for financial disputes the Oz Shepherd would be sent.

PRIVATIZATION OF GOVERNMENT

How the shepherds resolve these conflicts will impact the votes they get later from the cities or shires that were in conflict. To assist the shepherd in resolving such disputes, the shepherd may employ a member of the nobility (Royal Family) who is viewed as unbiased to assist in disputes. If the situation is escalating the shepherd may call upon the Prince of the Covenant. Dealing with these conflict resolution processes should give them some useful first-hand experience in dealing effectively with municipal disputes, and that, in turn, would also be useful if they should ever succeed to the position of Royal Finance Minister advising the Prince of the Covenant, who must have good techniques for dealing with conflicts between nations, and advanced diplomatic skills, to prevent wars and expand friendship and unity between nations and peoples.

In Section 2 I discussed migrating the House of Representatives portion of the US Congress directly to the people, however, to preserve the powers and authority of the shire governments the Senate, or the House of Lords in the British Parliament, representing the individual shire governments is also needed. As I eliminated the middleman in the House of Representatives to take the law-creating process directly to the people, our new House of Lords is exactly that, the collective power and vote of all the lords in the Kingdom. To accomplish this, each lord may submit one proposal to the other lords in the Kingdom. These proposals are limited to the following areas: How conflicts and general interactions between shires, as well as between shires and lords, and the realm and halo governments, to preserve shire sovereignty as well as the general evolution and operation of the shire government. New forms of taxation, as well as tax collecting method, are forbidden from such laws to ensure the rights of the public are not violated and to ensure the financial solvency of the realm and halo governments. After the lord submits a proposal, the other lords in the Kingdom may sign the proposal they like the most. The ones with the most signatures at various times will be sent to all lords. A town-hall meeting will be called for so that the people can voice their opinion. If a majority of lords ratify the proposal, it will be placed on the national Kingdom ballot. Passage will require a popular majority from a majority of Shires. Note this is different than a popular vote from the Kingdom, as it is possible to get a majority of Shires and pass the proposal without a popular national majority. This is allowed as we would not want the rights of rural communities and shires with smaller populations to lose their voice and atrophy due to the Shires with metropolitan population centers.

To preserve the autonomy and the local powers of the people a great deal of authority has been granted to the individual lords, however, we do not want the lords to assume tyrannical powers either as we saw historically in the Feudal system. In the Republic, this was accomplished through a divided authority structure, i.e., the city council, the state legislature, and the national congress. Legislatures, city councils, and other designs to divide leadership have many positive attributes because they restrain what one person may or may not do with the vested authority of a position as that may impact other people's lives. However, as this is implemented each of the constituent parts of these political entities naturally become less and less accountable for the decisions that were made by their group, as a matter of simple mathematics, as we pointed out previously. The key is to provide a way to maximize the strengths of divided-leadership, thereby ensuring that no-one person is given too much power, but at the same time keeping each legislator or council member directly accountable on an individual basis for every decision. Thomas Jefferson saw it this way: *It is not practicable for the executive branch of government to be headed by anything other than a single person. The president [or in our case the shepherd or lord] has advisors in the form of heads of departments, but the responsibility for all executive actions rests ultimately and finally on his own shoulders.*[20]

Jefferson, along with many of the original designers of the U.S. Constitution, had a puzzling dilemma, for they knew that they needed divided-leadership in Congress to prevent any one person from taking on too much power that rightfully remains with the people. Meanwhile, they also realized just as clearly that by dividing leadership, they were also losing tangible individual accountability. In this new and better system of truly democratic government, what we attempt is to receive the blessings of divided-leadership (as found in Congress) and the strong individual accountability of an executive, whether it be the lord on the shire level or the shepherd on the national level. To achieve this end, each lord is independently accountable to his or her city for the direction and vitality of that city, and this does not change even though the lord is also part of a larger group including the other lords of the Shire. By creating a legislature of lords composed of all the lords of each shire, we maintain their accountability while also apportioning their leadership among themselves. We will call this legislature the Shire Fellowship, which is fashioned after city councils as they presently exist, but this one will have similar duties operating at the shire level. The rationale behind this Shire Fellowship is to add that fourth restraint on the power and authority of lords while at the same time directly maintaining their full accountability. Thomas Jefferson referred to the Shire Fellowship proposition as *little republics*, referring to the lord as their warden, who also acted as the representative of each city, a.k.a. *ward* in the shire. He presented his plan this way: *My proposition [to divide every county (shire) into wards [cities] and to establish in each a free school] had for a further object, to impart to these wards those portions of self-government for which they are best qualified, by confiding to them the care of their poor, their roads, police, elections, the nomination of jurors, administration of justice in small cases, elementary exercises of militia; in short, to have made them little republics, with a warden at the head of each, for all those concerns which, being under their eye, they would better manage than the larger republics of the county (shire) or State. A general call of ward meetings by their wardens [lords] on the same day through the State (Realm), would at anytime produce the genuine sense of the people on any required point and would enable the State (Realm) to act in mass.*[21]

For several reasons, the Shire Fellowship, *our little republic,* is a vital part of the whole political design. There are several major needs too large for most individual cities to handle. At the same time if those needs are given over to the governments of the realms, then the public is no longer able to vote on its shire expenses in its shire

---

[20] In Defense of Democracy, <etext.virginia.edu/jefferson/quotations/>, Letter to William Stevens Smith (November 13, 1787), quoted in Padover's *Jefferson on Democracy*, <en.wikiquote.org/wiki/Thomas_Jefferson>

[21] In Defense of Democracy, <etext.virginia.edu/jefferson/quotations/>, Letter to William Stevens Smith (November 13, 1787), quoted in Padover's *Jefferson on Democracy*, <en.wikiquote.org/wiki/Thomas_Jefferson>.

PRIVATIZATION OF GOVERNMENT

voting, on things such as jails, militia, and street maintenance in unincorporated shire land (which is not part of a city, town or village). Yet each of these matters requires some form of funding. This, then, is why the Shire Fellowship is formed—or that, at least, was one of the reasons. The other reason is to retain the underlying, deep-rooted integrity of the people's vote. If the government of the realm was to control the voting process, this runs the real risk of elected members of one political party trying to manipulate the public vote to get more members of that party into positions of power. If the vote were managed on the city level, this runs the risk of attempted manipulation of the vote by the lords. On the other hand, if the vote, the counting of ballots, and other electoral needs, are handled by all the lords of the shire, through the Underdogs, then each lord has a built-in incentive to make sure that all matters about the voting are fair and proper. Still, most of the expenses for things such as police, schools, roads, and parks remain with the towns and cities.

As we look at the present United States huge blocks across each state uniformly exist within the same political party. Such as huge portions of the Midwest are all conservative districts, while the West Coast are primarily liberal. Thus, it is possible, and even likely that there will be shires through which all lords reside in the same political party. Under such circumstances if the minority believes there are acts of intimidation or voter malfeasance what options are available? Among the realms the Willow Wisp realm was designed to enforce the integrity of Jezreel. Should the Shire Fellowship fail to reach a consensus, or the underdogs are unable to reach an agreement with the lords, the Willow Wisp Shepherd may be called upon to arbitrate. Willow Wisp also has its own courts. Should the minority believe their voting process has been compromised the Underdog may seek the assistance of the Shepherd or Willow Wisp and/or its courts. Because the Willow Wisp Courts are national courts, they represent an unbiased court available to arbitrate between the two sides. While the jurisdiction will always remain local, if corruption is found charges may be filed against those responsible and depending on the level of corruption if the court deems it necessary a new election.

Historically, we realize that for the Shire Fellowship to be effective, it must have a representative lord for each of the groups that compose the shire. However, not all people live within the boundaries of a town or city. How, then, can we ensure that all the people are represented in the Shire Fellowship? To satisfy this need when large tracts of land are scarcely populated, the people there may collectively vote in a lord under the title of a *village*. For example, if in an area of twenty square miles or greater there are at least three hundred and twenty inhabitants; they may organize under the auspices of a village, allowing them to vote in a lordship representative.

As population density increases, the size of the geographical area that constitutes a village or town decreases, by possibly dividing two villages or perhaps more depending on the representative needs of the area, ultimately ensuring that the right to collective representation in rural areas is not abused. Through this method, the portions of any shire that are not represented under the jurisdiction of a city, town, or village should be few and far between. At the other end of the spectrum, if a shire were to be made up of one city of, say, nine million and five villages of approximately three hundred residents each. That would mean that the Shire Fellowship would be made up of one lord from the metropolis and five lords, one from each village, giving the villages an abnormally high representation in the rural towns and a suppression of the larger metropolitan city. To ensure equal representation, as a city prospers (we hope) and enviably grows to exceed allocated population density within a specific land mass size area that city must be given options to divide to maximize the city's representation. For example, if a city located on eight square miles becomes greater than 256,000 residents, the city must be given options to divide, and if a city consisting of four square miles becomes greater than 512,000 residents, the city must be given options to divide, and so on. Notice each time the population doubles the allocated land mass is divided in half. Of course, these divides will only work successfully when the people in each division feel more represented than they were previously, for this reason, the people, each within their respective parts must be given a choice to divide or to remain the same. It is important to remember democracy always works best through choice and never by force.

This method was developed to allow equal representation between urban and rural populations. This method, however, has several potential issues in a rural population. In the current setup, the smaller the population is, the larger the area is that we are framing under the term *village*. It is possible in these areas to have an area of fifty or hundred square miles in which only a population of three hundred, five hundred or perhaps a thousand reside, thus categorizing them as a village. However, as is typically the case within the boundaries of the village may exist five, ten or fifteen separate communities. These smaller individual communities we will be referring to as *enclaves*. It is possible that each enclave may contain thirty-five, fifty, or perhaps a hundred residents. Each of these enclaves feels a sense of loyalty to itself, rather than loyalty to our *village* made up of multiple enclaves. The problem with enclaves is that each enclave is typically not self-sufficient, but must rely on shared resources in the form of schools, police, courts to support itself economically. Unfortunately, this runs into opposition with our design of the city to allow each lord sole responsibility over the well-being of the city government. To apply the same standards for urban budgets as we do for rural amounts to attempting to put a square peg in a round hole. Rural and urban environments work differently, therefore to address these issues a great deal of autonomy has been allowed within the village boundaries so that the people within the village borders can determine how their village budget, as well as individual enclave budgets, should function with little or no interference from shire law. Therefore, by design, we are attempting to create an environment where each village will act and function as a *little shire* to a certain degree. For example, each enclave will have its own representative enclave lord. The enclave lord will have a voice in the decisions made in his enclave as well as the village fellowship. However, only the village Guardian will have a voice in the Shire Fellowship as a representative of all the separate enclaves. Unlike the Shire Ring Bearer, which we will be discussing shortly, the village Guardian will be elected from an election covering all the residences of the village. This is because unlike the Shire Ring Bearer, the village Guardian will need to have the strength of all the individual enclaves to wield the support of the collective village residence when fighting for their voice as a member of the Shire Fellowship. Our enclave lords and village lordship candidates, like city lords will have a budget and tax rate on the ballot. However, unlike a city lord, our enclave lord's budget will only be responsible for some police and infrastructure needs not covered by the shire or village Guardian. By contrast, the budget for the village Guardian will be responsible for higher-level police investigation of crimes, judges, and other court costs. As far as which infrastructure needs or other services are covered and which are not will be determined through the public village vote.

Education, K-12, too, is also handled much differently for rural populations. Often many small towns will have one centralized school because it is too expensive for each town to provide for its own school. To stay true to our democratic ideals, the people in these enclaves must have a say in how these schools are funded and operated. To ensure the greatest voice among city residents, these enclaves are to be divided into different school districts that may cross shire borders if the creation of a school district is agreed to by all the supporting enclaves or geographical area. The head of each school district will be managed by a *principal*, who like a lord is responsible for placing an educational budget on the ballot; however, unlike the lord, no surplus is required. This will allow the people a direct voice in the education of their children while maintaining direct accountability on the shoulders of the district principal.

Growing up with two sisters and one TV set there was always a dispute over what to watch. I liked the boys shows, Transformers, Ninja Turtles, and they wanted to watch the girly shows, Strawberry Shortcake. My parents would say let's have a vote. With a minority of one boy and a majority of two girls I always lost. For if direct-democracy is to be well-designed, the present *fifty-one percent majority rule* way of thinking needs to be overcome so that in every way possible it becomes a system of government that maximize the rights of all, and especially of the "cast-aside person," whoever that might be. To achieve these ends, all the lords of any certain shire need to have an incentive to represent well *all* the people in their city, and especially those whom the lord suspects did not vote for him on Election Day. Throughout our world—from the Philippines to Syria, to Venezuela—republics have been known to grant extraordinary rights to the majority political party and to discriminate against members of the minority or losing parties. Gradually, with the passage of time, this arrangement engenders corruption, which, among other abuses of power, has been known to result in rigged elections rather than fair ones.[22] The problem occurs when nations begin to become polarized along party lines, with some people in support of the current government and others opposed. For instance, we can see this disquieting political polarization right now in the United States. There is also another dilemma: Each lord is responsible for their specific city, but who will be responsible for the interactions between the realms and the shire and who determines under what circumstances the Shire Fellowship should be called.

If the public could vote into office such person representing the shire as a whole, then that elected official would have even more authority than the lords, and in that case, at least theoretically, the autonomy of the city would be dangerously compromised as that singular person attempts to usurp powers intended for the lords

---

[22] The Prince by Niccolo Machiavelli – <the-prince-by-machiavelli.com/>

to increase their own. Remember, most government structures known to humanity resemble a pyramid. By allowing the lords to put their own budgets on the ballot, the people have greater local control over the taxes they pay. However, if lords lose control over their budgets, and that power goes over to the shire, the people lose their rights over local taxation and spending. Our design's solution to both potential problems is to allow the lords of a shire with the greatest percentage of the vote an opportunity to be designated as the *Shire Ring Bearer*. This arrangement keeps each lord in competition with the others, with the hope of election to this office. This arrangement also makes every citizen's vote within the lord's jurisdiction count even more because the lords who most please their populations can be rewarded by being able to run also for Shire Ring Bearer. At the same time, however, there is also a significant limitation upon the power of the Shire Ring Bearer because this official will not be elected by the shire, and that limitation reduces his or her power base.

On the other hand, this setup has some potential flaws. For example, lords, especially in small towns, as well as well-experienced lords, often find themselves running unopposed and thereby getting all the votes. Therefore, several incentives are established for opposition lordship candidates to run for the office of lord, to encourage competition for election to the office during the general election. Some of these incentives you already know about, such as the granting privileges to the Underdog to appoint shire judges. Also, when the lord violates his budgetary restraints, the opposition Underdog may assume the office. Furthermore, by limiting the number of elected positions available, the struggle among candidates for the office of lord is amplified. However, even with these additional options, there will still be times when lords run for office unopposed. Therefore, the top ten percent, or at least the top three lords (with the greatest consensus of votes from their locale) will make the case for their candidacy to all the lords at the Shire Fellowship. If a majority of the lords cast a vote of dissatisfied with the available options, the lords may nominate their own candidates into the position. If a candidate has not been elected after three days' time, the candidate with the greatest percentage of the Shire Fellowship vote will take office. If still undetermined the one with the most seniority will take office. The lord who is elected by the Shire Fellowship will be given the Shire Signet Ring and thereby become the Shire Ring Bearer.

It should be noted that there is not a shire budget, because it is the responsibility of the realms to tie the nation together, while it is the responsibility of the lords to ensure their citizens are represented. Consider Wyoming, the least populous state in the US. It is simply not financially feasible for the shire governments to create a road, telecommunications, and power grid over such large areas of sparsely inhabited lands. If such a shire budget existed in such areas ninety percent of the budget would be consumed by the interconnectivity between the cities and even then, it would be insufficient for their needs. Thus, before such projects are undertaken, a representative from the shire is needed to ensure the shires voice is present in the process. The Shire Ring Bear is that liaison position. As we have stipulated each city budget is independent from the others, yet all these independent budgets need to seamlessly fit together in concert with the realm's activities within the individual cities. For instance, the Star Gate realm, responsible for transportation may wish to install an intercity transit system throughout the shire. The Phoenix realm may wish to upgrade and or expand the shires power grid. The Willow Wisp realm may wish to build a series of libraries and/or a university. Each time the realm will wish to interact with the national government the Shire Fellowship must be brought into the loop so that the best possible integration will be undertaken so that none of the citizens of the shire are left out. Having one liaison in the Shire Ring Bear gives the national government a singular contact to schedule Shire Fellowship meetings and related activities. Beyond that if there are internal disputes between cities for the placement of roads or other needs the Shire Ring Bearer may call upon a gathering of the Shire Fellowship or a joint townhall meeting between the cities in dispute. Finally, if any given realm is negligent in the needs of the Shire, while the individual city lord may call upon the realm to intervene, in the absence of an adequate response the Shire Ring Bear may submit the request on behalf of the Shire Fellowship so that adequate attention is drawn to the situation. The closest equivalent in a republic is known as the Speaker of the House, an equal member of congress, but with the ability to organize which votes take precedence and when and which bills go up for a vote.

In LA County where I grew up there is a total of eighty-eight cities, Riverside County ninety, San Bernardino County seventy-three, Orange County thirty-four. Given the complexity and number of people involved it will take time to develop a consensus on shire planning needs. Of course, the best result is when the realms and each fellowship are in continual communication. Prudence would suggest that plans are in place through collaboration with the realms. Urban planning dictates the needs for construction phases and priorities. All this will need to be accomplished before the shepherds break ground on any given project. Without proper planning the expectation the shepherd will adopt the directions of the Fellowship become increasingly remote.

Remember that the shepherd's budget is not static. Depending on the economy the shepherd's budget adjusts accordingly. Thus, shire fellowships that have a grand plan in place if the economy contracts the shepherds may have at their fingertips multiple avenues through which to immediately spur growth.

Beyond that the fellowship creates a location for communication and collaboration on internal projects by the individual lords beyond the jurisdictions of the realms. Yet the lords, by design have the most demands on their time of all people in Jezreel. Thus, it is expected to be a legislature like the United Nations where the lord will send a person to the fellowship to represent him on all matters, keeping him in the loop and asking for his direction on upcoming votes and related matters.

The Shire Fellowship was designed to assist in local zoning, internal border disputes, as well as interaction with the realm governments for the purposes of city planning. However, any legislature carries with it the threat of usurping the legitimate law creation process from the people. Thus, several safeguards have been put in place to preserve the rights of the people. First and foremost, the laws that dictate the abilities of the Shire Fellowship come through the people so that the people are at all times over the lords. Second, each time zoning laws are put into place through the Shire Fellowship the national realm courts related to the legislation in question will be responsible prior to final approval. Third, most interaction between the Shire

Fellowship and each realm are in the form of recommendations or advisory opinions. Because they make no law, but merely advise the realm in their undertaking of shire projects no actual law has been put in place, thus no threat exists. If the public believes a threat to their liberties exists, the courts are available to hear their case. If the sees an infringement on the rights of the people, they can revoke the Fellowship ordinance. If they see no infringement, they can pass the ordinance. Finally, If any ordinance is questionable in part or in whole, the courts can put the ordinance up for a city or shire vote in the next election depending on the affected parties in question. For instance, an ordnance may expand or retract a city borderline, the court may send to a vote from the city or cities involved, rather than a shire wide vote.

Yet for every rule we must make an exception. Among the propositions voted into law in California was the California Lottery. However, the electorate missed the fine print stating that all California Lottery production and machines were designated to a specific manufacturer thus giving them a monopoly over the entire lottery industry throughout the state. Shire laws may put in place minimum safety and durability standards, but coercive laws to force the realm to use a specific manufacture, technology, or model undermines competition and future technological innovation. Thus, if the realm believes local laws are requiring substandard parts, monopolistic practices, or price fixing the realm may take their case to the related realm court to prove their case. The same goes for businesses. Imagine if Detroit outlawed Toyotas or Hondas from driving through their city. The Star Gate realm, our department of commerce, also has courts to hear such cases. Thus, there are cases that I would deny to the authority of the local vote. For instance, if Georgia votes to reinstitute segregation, slavery, or lynching it would violate the Love Orb and thus would not be permitted and would get kicked out at the *Causa Enim Novo*. The autonomy between the shires creates other loopholes that must be addressed. If a person commits a crime in one shire under what conditions should the local police be forced to stop at the shire border and under what circumstances should they have the authority to pursue? If the crime were murder the answer is clear, but consider the south during the days of the underground railroad where southern slaveholders were demanding the government allow them to enter free states to retrieve their slaves? Unfortunately, I don't have a crystal ball to see into the future, however, in all cases my prayer is that the law of Jezreel will transcend into the law of love. There is a natural evolution to things as Allah has set in place at specific preordained times. There are things that humanity is just not yet ready for on this journey, but my hope is that humanity will transcend are vices one by one until we achieve our utopian society.

Time has a way of complicating things. Optimistically the cities will be ever increasing as will the population and with it will come new technologies of all sorts. As such things unfold the importance of the fellowship will increase as will the intricacy of its web. Are expectation being that in the beginning the focus will be on the individual lords as they tackle the internal needs of their cities. As the situation normalizes itself the lords will see what works and what doesn't. Ideas will be borrowed from other lords as the rough edges are made smooth. As the city governments mature lords will began looking at the bigger picture from across the shire. The fellowship will begin to form committees to resolve city border disputes, enlargements, retractions, and the formation of new cities. Other committees may be set up for transportation, water, flood control, sewers, etc. As needed, they will reach out to the realms for guidance and planning. Thus, what was a temporary ad hoc institution becomes common place and routine. As John Adams saw the evolution of humanity, *"I must study politics and war, that our sons may have liberty to study mathematics and philosophy. Our sons ought to study mathematics and philosophy, geography, natural history and naval architecture, navigation, commerce, and agriculture in order to give their children a right to study painting, poetry, music, architecture, statuary, tapestry and porcelain."*

Spring Cleaning

As a child throughout the year I would acquire clothing, toys, and other things. When it came time to clean up most were stuffed in the closet or under the bed to give the outward appearance of a clean room. As adults we have the tendency to box things up and put them in closets, attics, cellars, and the garage to get them out of site. There they often stay forgotten until perpetuity. Unfortunately, governments often work the same way as sludge and clutter builds up in the system, it gets tucked away and forgotten so that no one knows about it. For this reason, once a year my mother would do what she called Spring Cleaning. She would empty out every box to organize and sort everything into groups to determine what stays, what gets donated, and what gets thrown away. The same periodic need exists within government. To ensure the government gets its pay, the Oz shepherd is to perform routine audits of random city governments to weed out waste, fraud, and neglect. From time to time these audits will provide a deep dive opening every proverbial box to see what goes and what stays. The question comes into play who audits the federal government. The job of the president under the US Constitution is that of an administrator, not a legislator. This is why they had a separation of powers between the executive and legislative branches. For better or worse the designers of the constitution were significantly right of center. This led the political left to run as legislators in that they each argue for changes to the law of the land in alignment with their ideology and to represent their political base. While the right would argue the opposite, to undo any change and turn all departments of the federal government, outside of those specifically referenced in the Constitution, over to the private sector in line with the tenth amendment. To bring this new government into proper alignment with the intentions of the US Constitution, the Prince of the Covenant unlike the US President is separated from the departments of the Federal Government which I reference as realms. Each of the realms is under the control of a Shepherd, just as each of the cities is under the control of a lord or lady. And just as each lord is held accountable through the position of the underdog, each Shepherd is held in place by the Guardian of the realm. The collection of all Guardian's makes up the Prince's cabinet. Among these Guardians is the Guardian over Oz and among his tasks is to perform a full audit and deep dive into every realm of the government. With the assistance of the other Guardians, they are to open every proverbial box in search of waste, fraud, and abuse.

Even if nothing is found it will provide each guardian with insight into the nuts and bolts of the system amplifying their ability to fully carry out the duties of their office.

These tasks are typically carried out by the political right, which is why the Soviet Union failed to do this and thus it collapsed under the weight of its own bureaucracy. On the other hand, Javier Milei took a chainsaw to Argentina's government and saved his country in the process. I also believe most are familiar with the waste, fraud, and abuse that Trump uncovered through DOGE, i.e.: the Department of Economic Development. Audits are useful because if you want to find corruption it is said follow the money. No government should be responsible for investigating itself. Thus, in the US Constitution there is a separation between the executive and legislative branches of the government so that while the congress allocates and spends, the executive administrates to ensure the wisdom and efficient use of resources. By creating a separation between the departments and the Head of State, the Head of State acts as a police force to ensure funds are spent with integrity. The Prince is empowered to prosecute criminal financial actions but is unable to change the budgets going into these departments as these powers remain with the individual shepherd of each realm. However, raising awareness of the issues provides the public with an accurate picture of how each shepherd is doing at managing the governments resources under their jurisdiction. Also remembering that the Guardians are rivals of their respective Shepherds, the ideological divide provides them with more than a little incentive to scrutinize every action the shepherd makes.

Having said that, I am reminded of the wisdom of Jesus, *"If a fellow disciple sins, go and point out their fault, just between the two of you. If they listen to you, you have won them over. But if they will not listen, take one or two others along, so that 'every matter may be established by the testimony of two or three witnesses.' If they still refuse to listen, tell it to the church; and if they refuse to listen even to the church, treat them as you would a pagan or a tax collector.*[23] Politics is always in search of public ways to discredit their opponents. Its goal is survival and to obtain power. Yet, righting the wrong is better than punishing the sinner. From time to time, we all need a second opinion. My goal is not for the Guardian to look for ways to discredit the shepherd as an avenue to obtaining his own political power, but rather to give each Guardian a voice in the wellbeing of their realm. As it is said in the law, *Innocent until proven guilty.* I want a built-in assumption that the shepherds were naïve or unaware of the issues uncovered. Once the Guardians make their reports, it is the duty of the Prince to discreetly make the shepherds aware of what was uncovered. In a best-case scenario both the shepherds and the guardians would work together for the greater good.

It is important to remember that the office of the Prince of the Covenant is made to be the office of the Messiah. In fact, the Prince is but a steward of that office until the return of the King, who is Jesus the Christ. Thus, the office is made to preserve the integrity of the Kingdom. Here it is mentioned because of the authority given him to preserve the financial integrity of the Kingdom. For the socialist I will show how he is responsible for the preservation of safety and other standards and regulations. For the republicans he has his part in the integrity of the criminal justice system. Yet even

---

[23] Matthew 18:15-17.

PRIVATIZATION OF GOVERNMENT

here there is a separation of powers, in that to Joseph was assigned the people, which is why their nation was historically called Israel, while the executive remained with the tribe of Judah. Thus, the Prince has neither the law creation rights reserved for the people. Nor authority over any of the realms, which are elected positions by the people. The Shepherds themselves represent a barrier between the people and the Prince so that a separation is maintained between the rights of the people and the powers of the Prince. The representative of Jezreel, direct democracy, necessitates the Prince is not elected, not a politician, but a position made for a King born in a barn, an *average Joe* humbly designed to be an honest mediator without political affiliation so that he can have an open ear to all points of view. So that when a politician of noble stature is caught with their proverbial pants down the first reaction is not to expose it to the public which only leads to pointing of fingers and the political game.

However, this same Jesus that advocated for discretion, also forcibly drove out the money changers from the Temple when he saw that the name of Allah was abused for financial gain. So that if the shepherd, or any branch of government, is averse to correction and attempts to take actions to conceal the wrongdoing than the only course of action is to turn the situation over to the associated guardian to go public with the facts they know, so that the people may determine who is in the right and who is in the wrong. Consider the boil on the skin. It will not heal on its own. You must burst it releasing all its pus and ooze. In the same way for society to heal the grossest of atrocities must be exposed for all to see so that evil may be purged from society.

This leaves us with a final dilemma as to who will perform the spring cleaning of the office of the Prince and the Guardians under him. This responsibility falls to the priesthood under the law of LOVE. Religious penalties are among the harshest in society, therefore how such an audit is to be performed, and its consequences remain as determined by the High Priest and the priesthood under him in accordance with the Word of God upon the Prince. The Prince, however, is responsible for disciplining his own staff, including the Guardians. Such crimes must be made public and include punishments up to that of termination of employment. If the Guardian shall be removed from their position through discipline, cognitive impairment, promotion, or death, the next runner up from the previous election will take his place. Promotion occurs if the shepherd is removed from office. Provided no fowl play is involved, as the underdog is designated to replace the lord, the respective Guardian will be promoted to the position of Shepherd.

As for the High Priest and the Priesthood, they do not receive a salary in the same manner as monks and nuns. Housing, utilities, transportation is the responsibility of the respective realms under the Shepherds. The temple and religious events are provided under the budget of the Prince. This general breakdown of checks and balances is generally the same as you will see in the coming sections.

Social Stock Market

When we analyze the need for the national military and other national projects, we gain a renewed appreciation for the country's other vital responsibilities, such as care for the homeless and assistance to the victims of violent crimes. The kingdom must look after its own, but to meet the fundamental needs of the Capitalist, it must do so in a way that does not create a welfare state, but rather encourages and promotes entrepreneurship, self-determination, and self-reliance. To accomplish this, our priority must be to remove the shackles from business and the consumer. Fantasia has ten different elements, and as stipulated previously, fantasia may not charge the public for any aspect of the services, it is responsible for providing to the public. This means that all water, electricity, phone lines, medical, etc. are provided through the national government, and if the government fails to meet these needs businesses, the public at large can take them to court with a judge appointed by the party in opposition to the shepherd. Thus, the burden is taken off the private sector so that entrepreneurship can flourish, and the consumer has more of his or her resources to put back into the economy. One of the largest expenses for business is start-up costs, for environmental impact studies, water lines, electricity, etc. This makes it next to impossible for any entrepreneur to startup any new business, which in most cases is also his or her dream, thus chain stores that have already accumulated large amounts of capital can meet these needs, but the new ideas and entrepreneurs are pushed out of the market to satisfy the greed of the state and national government. Through Fantasia, these responsibilities are on the shoulders of the shepherds to encourage new competition into the marketplace and through Oz training for the latest economy needs are continually feeding the capitalist engine the labor necessities it demands. The national government has been divided into ten parts to maximize the competition between each Shepherd and competition has been introduced into their budgets so that through the election of the Shepherd, each candidate, being unable to increase revenue will be campaigning on how to utilize the funds they have to the maximum advantage of the needs of the kingdom with the least expense possible. This also means that the tax burden has been removed from both the business and the consumer. Thus more resources are channeled into the economy. The more taxes a business must pay; the fewer employees it can afford to hire. If a business is providing a tangible benefit to society and its managers reinvest all their profits back into the business, with such plans as upgrading the equipment or hiring additional help, or at least they have plans for such expansion within, say, in the next five years, there can be no socially valid reason for a tax on the business. At the same time, because of the national personal income tax, we may still be sure that the government is continuing to profit from these businesses and getting its legitimate share. I am not naive; I know that businesses have their ways of hiding income that should be appropriated as a part of the income of the board of directors can involve the use of company cars or airplanes or business trips abroad on cruise lines to exotic destinations where the actual *business* may consist of relatively short meetings. However, this form of government is a direct-democracy and the people through their vote will determine what exactly is considered income for the board of directors through the ballot box, such that corruption could be considerably reduced or even eliminated altogether. It is for these same reasons that the income of the lords and other government officials are not determined by their own vote as it is in Congress or other government institutions.   Our economic goal is to create a business environment that produces the greatest amount of efficiency for the people's prosperity and general well-being. If a business is taking in profit but can find no way to reinvest those funds (as if this would ever happen), then the public can mandate a portion of those funds to be allocated to charity.

The strength of any national economy is determined by calculating the total value of the goods and services it produces. When we analyze these goods and services, such as the construction of roads, houses, and industrial or agricultural commodities, we can establish a tangible benefit to society of these products. Yet there are other products and services such as the sale of cigarettes, alcoholic beverages, and salacious magazines that may adversely influence society in terms of its health, loss of work time, the quality of work performed, and be the cause of other social problems, such as domestic disturbances or rising crime rates. Still, in a democratic society, all persons must have meaningful opportunities to pursue their dreams, according to each person's own unique ways and rights to choose, even if it is in industries or activities that others, or even most people, might find in some way offensive or immoral. Remember, shires may allow, hamper, or prevent the growth and development of any industry or service, and this may be done through the popular vote, for to do otherwise would open the door of authoritarianism into this form of government. At the same time, we are aware—and it can be documented—that some goods and services do have an adverse general effect upon people. We know, for instance, that most sexual offenders have their desires inflamed by pornography. We know that substance abuse with alcoholic drinks increases domestic violence, and we know that drinking and driving absolutely don't mix—without the most disastrous and tragic of consequences, where lives are shattered forever, which is not only terrible for them but also passes the hardship along to society. We have also now the current debate out text messaging or other use of cellular telephones while driving. Who could count the cost for all the illegitimate children born to teenage girls? The kingdom now carries the financial responsibilities and counts the cost for these victims of crime and other highly questionable practices. These social offenders often require counseling, drug rehabilitation, or other public assistance, which, in the end, may amount to a huge drain on society's resources.

From our section for the humanist, you may recall that for direct-democracy, we designed a separation between those in society who are responsible adults and others who are dependents. We said that people not able to take care of themselves and live independently should not be part of the decision-making process that votes on laws because laws by their nature affect the lives of their friends, neighbors, and others in their community. This process was not intended to limit liberty illegitimately, but rather to enhance it. Society has, on many occasions, denied specific liberties, such as the consumption of alcoholic beverages during prohibition, because there are significant numbers of people who did not or could not use their liberties wisely. By creating a standard of acceptable behavior for independent, responsible adults, as opposed to others who are dependent, the hope is that specific extraordinary liberties will not be denied to society as a whole because of the inability of a few to use their rights wisely. Ultimately, which rights and liberties are granted and to what degree will vary from shire to shire, depending on the vote of the people.[24] We also realize that the level of dependency by degree will vary. For example, there are those who become aware that they have a problem and then seek help, and on the other hand, there are those who, due to their addictions and corrupted mental state have concluded by injuring themselves or ending the lives of others. Allowing this separation between dependent and independent adults allows society to create laws for less responsible, dependent people, regarding rehabilitation or other options for the greater, ultimate good of everyone.

Society has a responsibility to its weakest links for such services as counseling, rehabilitation, curing diseases (especially in cases of epidemics), and feeding the hungry. Under the governments of most republics, these responsibilities compose large parts of their budgets. For a direct-democracy, the question is, how can services for these elemental needs best be financed? The people are already responsible through their taxes for the local, realm, and national governments. Taxing businesses amounts to an indirect tax upon the people because taxes upon businesses push up the price of goods and services. Thomas Jefferson said it this way: *A wise and frugal government, which shall restrain men from injuring one another, which shall leave them otherwise free to regulate their own pursuits of industry and improvement, and shall not take from the mouth of labor the bread it has earned. This is the sum of good government.* [25]

In regard to businesses that thrive by exploiting our common human weaknesses, such as by producing recreational drugs or pornographic sexual entertainment (that tends to degrade and exploit women), by allowing the public to determine the tax rate on those industries we can discourage their growth, while at the same time find the means to provide funding to help the victims of such questionable organized activities, whether it be for institutional rehabilitation or by counseling from social workers. The question for us is who will be responsible for administrating these funds, the state or the private sector? History has shown that the cost-to-benefit ratio is starkly different between the private and the public-sector. The public-sector is made up of paid employees that typically have the job to provide an income for themselves and their families, whereas private sector charities are administered typically by volunteers who have responded to a calling and are attempting to make a positive difference in their communities, or for society.[26] Charities and other private humanitarian organizations survive off the donations from the public. By allowing the funds collected through the taxation upon these less reputable industries to be placed into charities and humanitarian organizations, and do so in a percentage equal to public donations, the public at large can determine, through its own giving, where those funds will go.[27] Whether these organizations are specifically religious or not

---

[24] Biblical quotes and reference logic <bibleresources.bible.com/bible_read.php> Levi (Matthew) 5:16, 7:1-6, 25:34-36; Torah (Deuteronomy 31) 184:7-13,
[25] In Defense of Democracy - <etext.virginia.edu/jefferson/quotations/>
Letter to William Stevens Smith (Nov 13, 1787), quoted in Padover's Jefferson On Democracy<en.wikiquote.org/wiki/Thomas_Jefferson>
[26] Hunger and Freedom in Ayn Rand's in The Voice of Reason- <capitalism.org/faq/poverty.htm>
[27] David Crockett, Charity and Congress – Advocates for self-government <theadvocates.org/library/christian-crockett.html>

may be a less important consideration than the humanitarian service they provide and how well they do it. Knowing that a person's charitable donation will be matched by funds from these types of businesses will encourage and add to those donations.

As disasters and other major emergencies occur, the average or ordinary people are the first to give. This is because such people are not bound by the same red tape as governmental agencies and corporate bodies. By taking government out of the equation, we remove bureaucratic impediments and allow the funds to get where they are most needed quickly and efficiently. The existing government programs now in place to help the poor consume a portion of the funds intended for the needy. By removing many intermediaries, a greater allocation of original funds allotted to those people in desperate situations will actually get there. The private sector, unlike the public, is always readily adapting to the changing situations within the economy. The public-sector, wherever there is a republic with capitalism and free-enterprise, tends to go on and on being unduly constrained by its original formulations. The private sector is inherently more energetic, dynamic, and readily adaptable, where inefficiency and waste must always pay a heavy price. For the public-sector to adapt suitably to these changes, requires an insurmountable effort with much cooperation and teamwork to get through its committees and both legislative houses before it arrives at the desk of the shepherd or the president. Even then, the governor or the president must sign the legislation before any true modification can be implemented. Thus, the public-sector process is for necessary adaptation slow and clumsy. This new donation strategy amounts to an attempt to amplify each dollar to be spent on assisting the poor and the needy. With an influx of this amount of additional funds to the private, charitable organizations everywhere throughout the kingdom, the benefit to those who are hurting would be gloriously exponential. In the same way, businesses are always looking for a new idea about a product to market; charitable organizations are always searching for a hurt in society to mend. Nobel Prize Winner Professor Muhammad Yunus explained the difference like this: *We need to reconceptualize the business world to make sure it contributes to the creation of a humane society, not create and aggravate the problems around us. One way to do it will be to create social business enterprises, along with conventional business enterprises, whose primary aim (unlike social business enterprises) is to maximize profit. Social business enterprises are a new kind of non-loss businesses, which aim at solving social, health, and environmental problems. Anyone who will go into business for the express purpose of human welfare we may call social business entrepreneurs. Many social business entrepreneurs exist today, but there is no mechanism to make them visible, no mechanism to bring them in-touch with individual investors who would like to invest in a social enterprise. Creation of a social stock market will be the logical answer to this matchmaking problem.*[28]

The government, in its own way through fines and citations, attempts to curb bad behavior. However, the funds received from these fines and citations in the present system are not used to benefit the victims that these fines and citations were created

---

[28] Social Business Entrepreneur, <muhammadyunus.org/content/view/56/83/lang,en/>

to prevent but rather used as a source of revenue for the government. In this new form of government that we are proposing these funds would also be proportioned among the various related charities as elected through public giving on a dollar for dollar ratio. For example, traffic citations could be used to pay for medical bills and rehabilitation of automobile accident victims. Hospitals and the healthcare industry, as well as many other organizations, could greatly benefit by transforming themselves into the kinds of social businesses of which Professor Yunus speaks. We can magnify charitable organizations to their limits, but unfortunately, charitable organizations will never be able to meet the everyday needs of social businesses for healthcare and other industries and services. Therefore, we created collective responsibility laws to provide for competition among social businesses through the city budgets. Our hope is to create an environment for competition among social businesses, not for maximum profit, but rather to achieve the maximum good for society. The role of the shepherd is not to ensure that the maximum amount of city spending goes into these programs, but rather to ensure that these programs live up to the standards demanded by the people through national law.

There are other benefits, as well. Often during times of war, under the present system of government, all financial resources are put into the effort to win the conflict at hand, but this often leads to cutbacks in other vital programs, including education and healthcare, and it is sad especially during wartime when veterans' disability funding is cut rather than increased. Shifting these social industries out of the national budget to the local budgets ensures their continued coverage during such times of need.

We seem to live in a government divided between solutions developed out of government itself and solutions that originated in business, but we need to remember that there is this third option. Our endeavor must be to create an avenue for funding for these social enterprises that originates with the people. Still, it should be one that allows for healthy competition between these industries and the public-sector, if we are to have a result amounting to the highest good of all. However, yet again, we run into an issue, the Social Stock Market is dependent on receiving funds from fines throughout the Kingdom to supplement their income. Some of these fines are from those levied against the lords if they attempt to use fraudulent methods of taxation, however, if the lords collect and report greater amounts of income and therefore greater amounts of tax revenue the Shepherd of the Oz halo created to collect tax revenue from the cities has the wrong incentive to look the other way and because his midterm election comes through the vote of the lords if he does enforce the law he may get punished from the lords for merely doing his job. For this reason, each Shepherd carries a different responsibility to enforce different laws. The Shepherd of the Fruit of the Spirit halo is responsible for the Social Stock Market to ensure that the lords are following the law, as if they are not those finds are reported to the Social Stock Market under that Shepherd. The Social Stock Market is made up of Nonprofit organizations all dedicated to the same goal of ending poverty. To win the midterm elections, the Shepherd of the Fruit of the Spirit halo must get a majority vote from the Social Stock Market companies who will evaluate the Shepherd's performance for a world in need. If the Shepherd does not enforce the

PRIVATIZATION OF GOVERNMENT

law against the lords who violate their tax restrictions, he or she risks being voted out of office and his competitor and runner-up in the previous Shepherd election, the Guardian of Entrepreneurship, will become the next Shepherd of the Fruit of the Spirit.

One of the problems Nonprofit and government institutions to help the poor is that often administrative and promotional costs out way the funds that actually go to those in need. Furthermore, of such programs often create an aura of dependency that tends to keep the poor in poverty instead of getting them out of poverty. In the United States, several welfare programs were created to help the poor, but ending those programs turned out to serve the poor much better. Several generations had gone dependent on those very programs, and so when people learned that their safety net was going to be removed, thousands of welfare recipients entered the workforce for the first-time. They received their self-esteem back, and a better person emerged, resulting in safer neighborhoods and a drop in the crime rate. The goal of the Shepherd of the Fruit of the Spirit is to end poverty by helping people help themselves to get out of poverty. Part of the fines that come into the Social Stock Market are from businesses fined for unethical practices, but we don't what the Shepherd, in his zeal to fund the Social Stock Market undermine the free-enterprise system responsible for bringing people back to work. Therefore, we allow the Guardian of Entrepreneurship two options for the Shepherds midterm election, either a Social Stock Market vote or a Stock Market vote from the CEOs of the Kingdom. The Guardian of Entrepreneurship is responsible for representing the business world, to see if poverty is truly declining or if the Shepherd is just merely creating an aura of dependency. A while back, I worked in a call center for GE Security. The managers and supervisors were paid and promoted by how many calls the employees under them took and how quickly they could solve each call. Under these conditions, if a person's issue was not solved and the customer called back, the employees were encouraged to open a new ticket. If the caller had to call in five times or six, this resulted in five to six additional tickets, which made the manager look good in the eyes of upper management as the call times were lower and the number of calls was higher. I was routinely reprimanded because I could truly resolve the customer's technical issue with one call, but typically, that call was longer than my coworkers, who did not solve the customer's issues. While customers liked talking to me better and often requested me personally, the managers denied my promotion because I took fewer calls, and each call tended to be longer. Often NGOs will boast of how many people they feed, or they clothed, but the real story is the story behind the numbers, and the real questions need to be asked to see if they are truly getting the poor out of poverty. Having said that I am not looking for a Shepherd that boasts to the Kingdom how many people he fed or clothed, but rather what is the story behind the numbers. This is the story the Guardian of Entrepreneurship is tasked with telling the Kingdom. There will always be desperate situations, and the Fruit of the Spirit is one of many halos of Fantasia always looking for volunteers that will provide shelter, food, and the necessities of life so that even here the work ethic is present. Due to the competition between these elements it is expected that greater benefits will continually be offered to the volunteers as each element of Fantasia struggles to attract labor, thus anyone who is willing to work in Jezreel will have a plethora of options available to them so that at any given time the entirety of the economy should be operating at full and maximum employment levels without reverting to a welfare state or anything closely resembling it.

Charity organizations, commonly referred to as Non-Profit Organizations or NGOs with all their benefits to humanity, still carry significant threats to society that cannot be ignored. Take any natural disaster, a hurricane, tsunami, earthquake, etc. images of people in distress flood television screens and websites and NGOs respond with a flood of food for those in need. Often the free food continues for months or even years. As the price of food drops to zero, the local farming communities can no longer receive a profit from the food they harvest, so they leave their fields behind in search of other professions. Without the local support, the population becomes dependent on the foreign aid and a welfare state is formed so that the solution to correct the problem, itself becomes a source of bondage. Two people fall down. One is bruised but has the ability to get up on his own; the other person has broken his leg. Obviously, the person who has broken his leg needs help because he is unable to get up on his own merits, but to help the person who can get up on his own, but chooses not to, is doing him a disservice by enabling his dependency instead of doing what is necessary for him to become independent. Under these conditions, the Guardian of Entrepreneurship becomes a vital part of the equation to ensure not only that people are taken care of, but that people are lifted out of poverty permanently by being able to take the reins of their own destiny.

The Federal Budget

If you have understood the government model of the shire as I have laid it out, then the national government should be easy to relate to as it is an expansion of that model on a national scale. The terminology used is different, but the purpose on each is the same. Just as the candidates for the position of lord are each required to submit a city budget the Wizard of Oz is required to submit a national tax rate as well as national domestic and foreign budgets every two years. Rather than reference the Wizard of Oz as a lord, we call him a shepherd. In this way capitalism through competition is not only brought to bear upon the local budgets, but the national budget as well. And just as we used the underdog to ensure that the lord was faithfully executing the responsibilities of his office, we have a position called the guardian, which is our second runner up shepherd to ensure the elected shepherd is fulfilling the duties of his or her office. As there are many lords that make up a shire fellowship, there are many shepherds that make up the Shepherds of the Roundtable. With me so far? If not, you may wish to read this last paragraph over again.

Yet there are still issues in the city budgets that I need to address. For instance, who pays for the underdog? If the underdog was provided out of the lord's budget, he has every incentive to push that portion of the budget to zero. The same is true for national underdogs, our guardians. For this reason, I am drawing a distinction and sovereignty between the national domestic budget and the national foreign budget. If you will recall the national domestic budget comes from the lord's mandatory budget surplus. The tax rate is made for the foreign budget. The foreign budget includes funding for military, embassies, etc. Now recall this is a kingdom, under the Prince of the Covenant, rather than an elected president. The prince is the head of the kingdom's foreign government, but like the US President is responsible for keeping the leaders of the domestic government in check. The prince's cabinet is made of the guardians, the underdogs of the national elections. This the prince can keep the shepherds in check without imposing his sovereignty over them. This also puts the prince, the guardians, and the underdogs, under the funding of the foreign budget, which is sovereign from the national domestic budget, as well as the local city budgets.

As I delve into the privatization of the federal government it is important to understand the objections of the capitalist to a democracy and how I plan to satisfy those objections while amplifying the voice of the people. Growing up I went on many camping trips with my cousins. My uncle and aunt would purchase candies at the local convenient store and distribute them equally among the kids. Within the first thirty minutes all the kids had devoured everything they were given. I, on the other hand, wanted to save mine so it would last through the weekend. However, because I was the only one with any candy left mine became primed. Left and right my candy was stolen by the other kids, and I was never able to appreciate even a single piece that year. The next year I learned my lesson. I didn't save anything. I gobbled everything up like everyone else. I knew if I didn't I would either lose it all anyway to theft or all the enjoyment of the trip would be lost in a continual struggle to protect my assets from the will of the majority. There are many who gain wealth in an economy through illegitimate means, but to paint all the rich with a broad brush is to deny the hard work of the millions who legitimately fought their way to the top through good old fashion hard work. Among my most common arguments against democracy is that the *'have nots'* who squandered their savings will vote to steal it from those who have earned it until everyone is poor because there is no intrinsic value to hard work and savings. Just as occurred between me and the *'democracy'* of my cousins. To preserve the liberty of the capitalists, checks on the power of national taxation are necessitated. Conversely, I must also consider things such as America's Military Industrial Complex, whereby the rich through their wealth use lobbyist to funnel the publics taxation dollars back into their own pockets. To fully appreciate these checks and balances, we begin with how the national military is funded. The federal budget to fund the military, the Prince, the Guardians, and the like, is designed in much the same way as the city budgets are designed for cities. In the same way that lordship candidates put their budgets on the ballot, the candidates for the Shepherd of Oz each submit a national budget on the ballot. Yet spending at the national level is obviously a different matter than local spending. There are also other basic comparative differences, such as, for example, there are times when a country may find itself at war and the spending levels of the kingdom, for its own preservation, need to be changed quickly and drastically.

When we analyze spending on a local level, we know that there will be cities in which most of the people are poor, and there will be cities where most of the people are rich. If there were to be a divided tax structure based on higher tax percentages for those with higher incomes, because of these tax rates, we would be encouraging the rich to live apart from the poor. When done on a national level, however, this is not the case, for the concept of allowing the people to choose their own tax rate really does bring about choice in taxation. The challenge with a divided tax structure is that this allows those who pay less to determine which tax percentage someone else will pay. There will be people who vote for higher taxation not because they believe it is in everyone's best interests but only to punish the wealthy (i.e., out of resentment). In Europe and elsewhere, there have been extreme examples of the very rich being required to pay as much as One-hundred and five percent of their income back into the government coffers. At the same time, we need to analyze the practical aspects of a divided tax structure. The top ten percent of American wage earners pay a full sixty-three percent of all taxes collected.[29] This means that if the national government were to be forbidden from taxing the lower ninety percent of all wage earners, it could still get sixty-three percent of the taxes it normally collects. Of course, under this direct democracy, the national tax is responsible primarily for the foreign needs of the nation, rather than the national domestic needs of the kingdom, which is the responsibility of the Roundtable, and the Roundtable receives most of its funding from the lordship budgets. Moving on to the next step, we discover that the top five-percent of wage earners pay roughly fifty percent of all taxes collected.[30] We know also that as the tax percentage rates increase, at some certain point, the profit received from the percentage rate declines.

To help explain this better, consider your own budget and the budget of your friends. Some people in society make a lot of money and can afford to put that money into homes and luxury items, but other people just make enough to meet their immediate needs with nothing leftover. This is the way businesses work also. Some are large and make huge profits allowing them to grow and expand, but others are lucky to just break even. Hypothetically, let's say the tax rate was one percent. This means that government represents roughly one percent of the economy, and the private sector represents roughly ninety-nine percent of the economy. Because the government is dependent on the private sector through taxation to fund itself at one percent, the government is receiving that one percent from ninety-nine percent of the economy. If the government were to raise taxes to two percent, there would be a small portion of businesses that were just breaking even at one percent taxation that would now go belly-up due to the higher tax burden. With two percent taxation, the government portion of the economy grows, and to meet the government demands the government hires more people, which take people out of the business sector. This means that taxation collected at two percent is greater than taxes collected at one percent, but it does not double the income because the taxes collected come from only ninety-eight percent of the private sector as the private sector is now smaller than it was previously. Each time taxes increase, the return on the profit from that taxation diminishes, until increasing taxes actually lowers the government's total revenue. Business represents the products-and-services-creation portion of the economy. The higher the tax burden, the smaller ratio of business-to-government economy there is. Unfortunately, this leads to other harmful consequences because having fewer industries means fewer goods will be available

---

[29] U.S. tax analysis for 1999

[30] U.S. tax analysis for 1999

for purchase. This ultimately equates to higher prices for the average consumer for goods received. Also, we must consider the demands for the most basic needs: food, shelter, transportation, etc., the proportion of which increases as the person's income diminishes. Of course, we realize that many factors can contribute to the success or failure of an economy. However, it is important to mention that historically within the United States each time the tax level has been cut significantly, the tax revenue coming into the government increased. We see this in the Coolidge administration, the Kennedy administration, and most recently in the Reagan administration.[31]

To maximize the productivity of the economy, taxation on most people and the bulk of the economy should be lowered, especially where the demand is the greatest on the lower end of the spectrum. To meet these needs, we produce maximum taxation amounts among different taxation percentages. For example, any person making less than the top ten percent of wage earners will not have to pay any federal income taxes. For those at the top five to ten percent, they will not be taxed on the national level until their income has gone above the top ninety percent of taxpayers, and then their national tax may not be greater than ten percent of their income. For those at the top one to five percent, their tax may not be greater than twenty percent of their income, and so on. This is not to say that these rates are going to be the tax that is charged, but rather that no higher percentage of taxation may be charged. Surprisingly, in 1999, the top 1 percent of all wage earners paid 29 percent of all taxes that were collected. For these top wage earners, they may not be taxed at a rate greater than 35 percent.

During the Great Depression, the divides between the rich and the poor created a great deal of animosity between the poor and the well to do. The FDR Administration felt if these concerns were not addressed the foundations of the American system of government may fall prey to the path of communism. To help alleviate tensions income taxes of ninety-four percent were enacted on incomes greater than $200,000, with inflation in today's dollars that would be only income that was greater than twenty million dollars a year or more. The income tax system established by FDR was never intended to be levied against the middle class or the poor. However, without constitutional restraints, the long arm of the government eventually stretched into everyone's back-pocket. With the passage of time soon, taxation trickled to the middle class and then the poor. Today even Social Security checks are taxed. It was John Marshall, Virginia Delegate to the original constitutional convention and Chief Justice of the US Supreme Court from 1801 to 1835 who originally warned, *"The power to tax is the power to destroy."* These constitutional safeguards have been put in place to prevent this trickle-down taxation from eventually eroding the freedoms and foundations of the direct democracy from within.

The only tax percentage rate where all such barriers are to be removed is the top point one percent (0.1%). History (e.g., the French Revolution, 1789-1799) teaches us that the poor will, at some point, revolt when the gulf between the rich and the poor becomes too great. By removing barriers for high taxation from the top 0.1 percent—that is, the top one out of a thousand wage earners—we create a release

---

[31] Econ 101: How do tax cuts work? Business and Media Institute, <businessandmedia.org/commentary/2006/com20060111.asp>.

valve on the pressure that may build up with the passage of time between the rich and the poor.[32] We know that the wealthier people in societies of the past, due to their wealth, often have had a greater voice in government. Allowing the people some control over the tax percentages of the very wealthy allows them to act, when necessary, as an appropriate contrary force.

The first element in promoting capitalism is a good reputation among your potential consumers. The BDS movement (Boycott, Divest, and Sanction) paid a heavy toll on American businesses that even showed the hint of support for the genocide in Gaza. After the name of these businesses were tarnished the perceived blood on their hands the stain was one that no matter how many times they washed, it would not be remove from the minds and hearts of humanity. In foreign affairs, when corporations unfairly exploit people abroad, those people may take their grievances to the House of God Courts as a way of exposing extortion, monopolies, or other unfair business practices. In America humanity saw the business sector exploit the most impoverished nations of the world for their cheap labor and resources. And when those governments attempted to object, they were overturned through covert actions by the CIA or American armed forces. However, it may be difficult to change the way other countries behave, but we may choose to alter the way our government responds to the covert or auspicious actions of other nations in ways that are more sensitive to the people living in those nations. In foreign affairs, our long-term goal should be to reach the people of other nations in more positive ways and to improve mutual understanding. If their people—rather than their governments—do approve of our kingdom and its people, that will be a major step towards good relations and mutual prosperity.

The best way to restrain the Military Industrial Complex is to deny it of funds. Because funds for Fantasia come through the flat tax from the city budgets, then everyone becomes subject to taxation. This would also mean that all the citizens of the kingdom would have a strong incentive to keep taxes as low as possible. Since the primary responsibility of the Prince of the Covenant is the national military, this also means that the national military must remain as small as possible. Because the Shepherds of the Roundtable contain the available surpluses of funds for war, the Prince of the Covenant will be directly dependent on them for approval of any military funds. Of course, this means that the tax burden on the lower ranks of society would be significantly greater, and funds available for national projects would be significantly less. This would also mean losing our pressure gauge on the wealthy in times of major economic stress. History tells us that during trying times, the people look to the national government for solutions. Any attempt to remove a divided tax system risks undermining the national evolution of government funding, and therefore also of undermining the government itself. When the candidates for Shepherd of Oz are running for office, even with a divided tax structure, we should still expect that the candidates will get pressure in some way from the people to keep taxes as low as possible.

---

[32] Jeremiah 22:13–17.

PRIVATIZATION OF GOVERNMENT

At the same time, we must remember that these national income taxes fund the national military and other foreign-relations needs. In times of peace, the need for a large national military and military spending is low. It seems logical, then, that we can expect the Shepherd of Oz, when running for office, to want to use such funds domestically, inside of the kingdom. The challenge is that while the Shepherd of Oz submits a tax rate and budget, the funding is divided between the domestic budget under the Shepherd of Oz and the federal budget under the Guardian of Oz. The Roundtable is responsible for determining foreign military risks abroad. Think of it as a dial. As the dial turns toward war the funds shift to the federal government. As the dial turns toward peace the funds turn toward the domestic government. All the shepherds' function through their domestic budgets, thus putting the Prince in a vote of ten to one. However, the shepherds also realize that war risks losing it all. My hope is that this will keep the military industrial complex in check looking for economic and diplomatic solutions, but also provide sufficient funds to provide for the existence of the national military. This also provides a foreign deterrent to war, as foreign countries realize any provocative actions will only accelerate a military build up within the Kingdom.

There is an old saying. If you want to hear God laugh, just tell him your plans for the future. Time has a way of changing everything. During times of war, economic downturns, national disasters, or other major crises, larger amounts of domestic funding may be urgently needed, and during those times, every dollar will count. As you may recall, the Shepherds of the Roundtable will retain part of the surplus of the lords' budgets in anticipation of economic fluctuations. Similarly, as with the lords, the Guardian of Oz will be required to lay aside sixty percent of the national taxation received as a surplus. On the national level, the plan will also be utilized for a regular surplus, except that instead of using it only for economic fluctuations, it will be used also for trade-off funding between military readiness needs through the Guardian of Oz and domestic national projects under the Shepherds of the Roundtable. All nations have choices within their national budgets, and during times of peace, they should concentrate on their domestic needs, whereas during times of war, those funds are channeled into the military. This is natural, according to the apprehension, felt among the public. Thomas Jefferson echoed this sentiment when he said: *In times of peace, the people look most to their representatives [the domestic government]; but in war, to the Executive solely... War requires every resource of taxation and credit.* So then, it is logical to imagine a divide between foreign needs and military readiness on the one hand, and domestic needs, with national projects, on the other.

National Projects

We mentioned that as a republic grows in population, the number of government projects undertaken decreases in size and scope but increases in the sheer number of projects, which means, from a political point of view, that then each congressperson can still send some money back to his home district to please the constituents. Unfortunately, this has led to several challenges because the projects tend to be of the type that should have been undertaken and constructed by municipal or state governments, such as colleges, hospitals, and libraries. To avoid this situation, shepherds will be limited to no more than five projects. This precaution will ensure that the projects undertaken will be larger, and in that case, they will tend to be beyond the funding capabilities of private businesses or shire governments. This arrangement will also mean that the shepherds will not have the sole rights to each project. In republics, it has been discovered often that elected representatives succumb to the temptations of accepting kickbacks and illegal contributions when they manage to bring a project into one area rather than another. By having many Shepherds of the Roundtable involved with these decisions, each shepherd must learn to compete and cooperate fairly and effectively about the funding. Our plan is, then, that shepherds who failed to get the projects for which they were hoping will be watching carefully and noticing how the shepherds who succeeded used those funds, whether efficiently and wisely, or poorly and to little purpose. By having the Roundtable approve the projects, each project should well reflect the needs of the kingdom rather than only those of some individual district, as now tends to be the case in republics. In addition, when the number of possible projects is more limited, which projects the country needs the most will be under discussion by the public, and in the news media, on the Discovery Channel, etc. If the shepherds want the support of the people, they will attempt to get the people involved in the selection process that will determine which projects eventually will be funded.

Historically, looking back on large-scale national projects in which America has been involved, from the Panama Canal to landing on the moon, we must realize that some projects may take longer than one-term in office to complete. We speak of not only past generations but also future generations as the Bible speaks of the transformation of the planet where seas are no more,[33] to provide the population with greater amounts of freshwater for growth among other things. The two that were mentioned for this new Genesis project specifically were the Red Sea and the Arabian\Persian Gulf,[34] such that they would be cut-off from the ocean through the construction of a land barrier the salt water removed and fed fresh water from the Nile, Jordan, Tigris, and the Euphrates respectively,[35] which will be accomplished before the coming of our Royal Highness in the clouds.[36] The Bible also speaks of other projects huge intercontinental mass transit system connecting Africa, Asia, and Europe.[37]

Then there are the possibilities within our own solar system. Consider the Electric Engine. It has a magnetized center rod running through the middle. On the outside magnets are placed around the rod, but not touching it. As electricity is pushed through the magnets the rod begins to spin. The greater the amount of electricity the faster the spin. Depending on the flow of the current the rod will spin forward or in reverse. Correspondingly each planet has a magnetic rod going from its north to south pole generating the planet's magnetic field. The moons surrounding each planet also spin through their magnetic fields though they are considerably weaker in power. However, if you ran a cable through a moon's magnetic core you could magnetize it, thus allowing you to increase, decrease, or reverse its planet's rotation. As the speed of the rotation increases so does its magnetic field. By manipulating the

---

[33] Revelation 21:1.
[34] Isaiah 11:15.
[35] Ezekiel 47:1-12; Isaiah 11:15.
[36] Revelation 16:12.
[37] Isaiah 19:23; 11:16.

flow and power of the current you can change the way it interacts with the planet's magnetic field slowly pushing its orbit either closer or further from the sun.

Now let us consider a new heaven and earth as Divinely foretold through the prophets. Venus and the rocky surface of Uranus are roughly the same size as Earth. By redirecting both planets orbit into one that a suitable distance from the sun you could make them both compatible for human life and creation. The gas giant Uranus has sufficient water to create oceans and an atmosphere for both Venus and itself. Though Venus has an excess of Carbon Dioxide, when water and heat conditions become ripe for spores, molds, and fungi they could soak up the excess Carbon-Dioxide in the atmosphere, thus making the temperature compatible with the plant, animal, and human life on its poles. While Venus does not have the seven moons of Uranus to assist in its rotation, moving Mercury into its orbit could serve as its moon for Venus. Naturally, projects of such a scale would complicate the process due to their longevity. Yet this does not diminish their value for humanity. What project could equal the value of creating a second and a third earth for human colonization? Nevertheless, longer projects move the responsibility to complete them to future administrations who may or may not see those projects as high priorities. The first step in ensuring that future administrations will complete projects is securing public support. For this reason, to ensure that the public genuinely is behind an especially large project, such major projects will require a public vote of approval, and we envision that especially large-scale projects will be the exception rather than the rule, knowing that such projects will require more time, effort, and resources. Any project large enough to require a national public vote will be counted as three projects. Thus, by this plan, the maximum number of projects will be limited to one large-scale and two normal-sized projects, or two large-scale projects in all. This means, then, that if the Roundtable submits one large-scale project, it loses three regular projects as well as running the larger risk of a *no* vote from the kingdom.

These projects will amount to a large portion of national funding. A threat too great to be ignored would be allowing Shepherds of the Roundtable to set aside whatever national project desired without considering the infrastructural and other needs of the kingdom first and foremost. Therefore, national projects must be limited to the country's internal needs. While shepherds may approve projects, they may select them only from projects submitted to them by a group; we shall call the Commission of Structural Engineering, to be discussed in the next chapter. National Projects submitted by the Commission of Structural Engineering will be limited to four general areas: science, technology, infrastructure, and exploration. This is done so that national projects will be focused primarily on national structural and infrastructure needs. This rule also creates a barrier between the shepherds and the Prince of the Covenant about the use of such funds. To maximize efficiency and speed, as well as reduce the projects' costs, the individual parts of the projects will be, as much as possible, bid out to the private sector. One of the special difficulties about a republic is that a congressperson may allocate funds for a project, but that person has no real authority to ensure that these projects stay within their allocated budgets because the authority to prosecute remains with the president, but ironically the president has no real ties to these projects. Typically, in a republic funds are allocated to the local community to see that such projects are completed, and these funds that reach local communities serve to benefit the community monetarily in terms of employment and local income. Nevertheless, without proper accountability, these projects sometimes spend four or five times more than the original bid, and this discourages honest companies from submitting a proper bid, or any bid at all, in the first place. However, on the contrary, our plan for direct-democracy makes the shepherds responsible for keeping each lordship budget under control to maximize the shepherd's total available resources for realm funding. The companies that undertake the actual construction of the projects in the democracy should be no different in this case from the lords because shepherds, unlike congressional representatives, have all the resources and the real financial incentives they need to ensure that these projects are completed on time and within budget. With this plan in place, if these projects were to fall below budget and ahead of schedule, these developments would open resources and options for future projects. Ultimately, this typical struggle between the shepherds and business contractors to cut costs and reduce project time is, in business terms, healthy, and it works to improve the general quality of life.

These projects, because of their size, scope, and nature, will be debated considerably in the public arena. Any significant loss of funds for these national projects will lower the number of projects that can be done, as well as their size and scope. This means that should the Prince of the Covenant take funding from the national project budget for military readiness; every dollar will seem important because the public will see and know the choices and will also understand more clearly what is being lost. Therefore, each increase in military funding will become subject to intense public debate. This accomplishes two things: First, it ensures that all the people will be behind the decisions of the Prince of the Covenant, and second, it sends a message to foreign powers that the country is seriously concerned about certain international situations and willing, if necessary, to become engaged. It also uses the media itself, through the discussion and debate process, to clarify the rationale behind any military buildup.

In today's shrinking, always more interconnected world, wars typically do not happen overnight. Usually, the country's foreign-relations experts can foresee dangers, and they have some understanding of rising tensions around the world, if not always an intimate understanding of all their causes. We refer to this kind of tension as the *national level of elevated risk,* which is to be an official measure of the degree of tension with the threat of war felt nationally. If there is no tension, then the sixty percent surplus from the Prince of the Covenant's budget will belong to the Shepherds of the Roundtable and may be used for national projects. As the international tension level or fear of war rises, the Prince of the Covenant may increase the nations elevated risk level thereby the percentage of the surplus available for the national projects decreases as military funding increases. The reverse is also true. What these arrangements do is provide the shepherds with financial incentives to push the Prince of the Covenant towards peaceful solutions to challenges abroad. At the same time, if they wish to enhance their popularity with the people, when the threat is real, the Shepherds of the Roundtable will have strong incentives to go along with the Prince of the Covenant. As the threat increases, the Prince of the Covenant may increase the elevated risk level further, and in this way, should war come, the kingdom will be ready.

Each area of Fantasia was designed to study a specific area of technology. Each Shepherds will have technological advisors, i.e., white mages, to advise them on the latest technological breakthroughs of the modern era. Cloud city, for example, studies the air, Atlantis the water, the Federation of planets, space, etc. In turn, each of the Guardians will have black mages, their corresponding military equivalent, Cloud city, fighter jets, the Federation, missile defense, Atlantis the navy, etc. so that the maximum technology is brought to bear on the national defense and vice-versa. Ergo as the level of elevated risk shifts resources can be immediately shifted between the shepherds and the guardians who manage those corresponding elements, however, with each increase in elevated risk the power and authority over Fantasia also shifts from the shepherds to the Prince thus if any war is not in the survival interest of the kingdom the shepherds will search and push for peace.

Among the strengths of capitalism over socialism is that it offers a financial incentive for hard work. That incentive, however, can be used to do all manner of evil because business will do anything for profit: right, wrong, legal, illegal, etc. Carl Marx once joked, *The capitalist would sell the rope to his own hangman because it was profitable for him to do so.* For this reason, the humanist ethical component through Jezreel or the moralist ethical component through the Prince and the Levitical Courts is a necessity for every aspect of the Kingdom. Thus, ethical components are discussed before the logistical ones: capitalism or socialism. The moral components help us guide humanity to what is right while the logistical components are as building blocks to reach our desired destination. The military industrial complex functions through the morality of capitalism without ethical boundaries, but purely to obtain and grow power. When a nation wields the power of destruction it can coerce weaker nations as humanity descends into its survival of the fittest primitive anarchy origins. When faced with a bully, there are two good ways to deal with him. First, a person can start talking tough in hopes that the bully will back down and be scared away. Second, it may be necessary to fight. Wars often start between an aggressor nation, a bully, and a smaller nation, the victim. As a war progresses, people worry about loss of loved ones, economic and financial situations. Even the hint of war can be unsettling and, in some way, is felt by each person in the kingdom. Raising the official level of elevated risk will be viewed by other nations, as a prelude to war, and for the Prince of the Covenant, taking this action is not a decision that should be made lightly. The Guardians words before the people will be well thought out and made to not only be heard internally but also abroad. This is the courage and tough talk we hope will call the bully's bluff. Taking this before the public will cause anxiety and may cause some to panic, but to keep the people ignorant of the dangers would be to suppress the natural goals of direct democracy, which trusts the people. Democracy is not designed to be easy upon the people, or undemanding, but as a responsible way to freedom and the people must learn to take upon themselves their actual responsibilities for the many challenges that there will be. Our inspiration could be the final line from the "Star-Spangled Banner: *"The land of the free and the home of the brave."*

Economization of Socialism

Considering the harish realities of war in the next section dedicated to the socialist I am going to delve into diplomacy and international relations. Our current world order is run through a capitalistic model of competition between nations. On an international level this competition has led us into two world wars. Beyond that, international laws, such as the Geneva Convention, are routinely violated as witnessed in Gaza, the West Bank, and Lebanon, because enforcement is voluntary, dependent on competing sovereign states upon whose best interest compels them to look after themselves alone and look after others only when it is in their best interest to do so. The League of Nations failed to prevent World War II and under the watch of the United Nations humanity has been unable to prevent a live televised genocide as it is hamstrung through a veto power that declares might makes right as any semblance of international law crumbles away toward international anarchy. Solomon said there is a time and place for all things under heaven. There is a time and place for capitalism, but I want to submit to the capitalist that there is also a time and a place for socialism. Rather than a world of competing nations, I am going to put forward a framework for a family of nations where the borders between nations are gradually blurred and then erased all together. Thus, in the next section I will be delving into the international government of diplomacy, alliances, trade, and related topics.

Among the books that follows the socialist is dedicated to the liberal through a national government that is created around their needs. In that book I am going to discuss the roles of each of the shepherds and how I plan to use them to represent the domestic national government. There are vital components within every nation that by their nature represent a monopoly of power, such as the interstate freeway system and the power grid. In America there is also a great debate over universal healthcare. If you are in a car accident and you are in danger of imminent death, is that a good time to shop around for the best medical system? The framers of the US Constitution used Adam Smith's guide, *the Wealth of Nations*, a great deal in its design. According to Adam Smith the great enemy of capitalism is monopoly. The framers saw the presence of a corporate mail delivery system as a potential monopoly and upon his advice nationalized the US Post Office. Today capitalistic monopolies have failed capitalism in real ways. Thus, ironically, I am going to utilize the concepts of Adam Smith, the founder of American Capitalism to create a federal government based on socialism. Any who look at the American government would point to socialisms failures, but these failures exist, because socialism was injected into the framework of a constitution that was not created for its existence. My goal with all the philosophical elements is to meet and exceed their dreams beyond their wildest imaginations. This is equally true for the socialist as it is for the capitalist.

Does this imply I am creating a socialist national government in opposition to the needs of the capitalist? Far from it. My approach has always been and will always be to create a symbiotic relationship between the philosophies, so that while they are in competition with one another, they will also amplify one another. For instance, imagine a private sector that no longer had to pay for health insurance, water, power, or communications. A private sector where profits are reinvested into the business, not demanded by the state through the force of taxation and without the burden of having to grease the hands of government bureaucrats in Washington D.C. in the form of campaign contributions in order to do business. This is hard to believe that nationalizing universal needs will result in a tax burden upon the private sector that will be less. This is because while in a republic socialistic and liberal programs seemed to have no cap on spending, but continually have their hand out with the demand to continually give more through the force of taxation. In my new democracy because the people will approve their budget and public taxation this is not the case. Utilizing free market principles, a request for increased taxation, must be justified to the public to provide a better service or the people will vote against it. As you will recall this new economic system uses economic cycles to create an intentional situation which will encourage one side to expand, and the other side is forced to contract. Forcible contraction amplifies the need for efficiency in both the capitalist and the socialist. The problem in America is that the business sector has the ability to fail which forces them to economize drastically, while the socialist aspects of America are shielded from failure through continual deficit spending and forced taxation from the private sector. If a business in the private sector is inefficient and the quality of their output is poor, they will go out of business, but socialist programs often continue irrespective of the quality of their performance or product produced. Thus, without incentive to improve performance or quality the bureaucracy takes continually more while producing less. This was the set of circumstances that brought down the Soviet Union. This new system of the federal government, I call Fantasia, alters the environment of the socialist and the liberal into a position where they are forced to utilize socialism, not capitalism, to enhance efficiency and productivity and face real consequences from the public for failing to meet the need demanded from them. Also consider while the private sector is in competition with its rivals that produce similar products and services but is also dependent upon the private sector to purchase the tools and raw materials needed for the business to function. In this new socialistic system, there are several sovereign realms of socialism, each independent and in competition with one another for funding so that they are not attempting to get more funding from the public through taxation but with existing funds amongst themselves. And while they are in competition with one another they also are forced to rely on one another in a symbiotic relationship to function, for if one fails, they all fail and thus they all lose. Thus, in this sense, I am utilizing the principles of Adam Smith to maximize the efficiency of socialism through an experiment of American Socialism. Not in modern terms, but the lost ideals as seen through America's founding fathers. The capitalist may not believe this, but if done correctly, the socialist can be exponentially more efficient than the capitalist. Because the socialist system is not based on declining profits, but the needs of the human family. As the capitalist aspects of this system forced lords out of office who did not meet their budgetary restrictions, so to the shepherds of the socialistic realms that are unable to meet the needs of humanity will face the wrath of the people. So for the conservatives and libertarians reading this in disbelief, remember this, as liberal and socialistic as I create the national government, unlike a republic where spending seems endless, our socialists and liberals to advance will be forced to optimize every dollar. As we move on to the socialist and the liberal the evidence of this will be understood. Remember my goal is to accomplish the impossible. To my liberal and socialist friends, you are vitally important to me, and your books are coming!

www.ingramcontent.com/pod-product-compliance
Lightning Source LLC
Chambersburg PA
CBHW080952170526
45158CB00008B/2452